LOST WARRIORS

STORIES OF INDIA'S UNSUNG HEROES : 15 GREAT WARRIORS OF ANCIENT AND MODERN INDIA

ARIN KUMAR SHUKLA

Dedicated to all warriors, known or unknown, who

sacrificed their lives defending

Bharat...

and

In loving memory of my grandfather,

Umashankar Shukla

Contents

Preface

Bharat... The land of the brave, abode of the mighty. This soil has given birth to brave sons, and the heroes have paid the debt of this soil with their blood. Ram-Krishna played in this soil, and brave Arjuna also practiced archery in this soil. In this soil, many successful heroes sacrificed themselves for the sake of their pride, but got caught in the shackles of time and history. History has sung the praises of invaders and opportunists who came in the place of these heroes. From Chhatrapati Shivaji Maharaj to Maharana Pratap, and from Emperor Prithviraj Chauhan to Chakravarti Raja Raja Chola, this nation is indebted to each and every hero who laid down his life for the glory of this soil. This book is an opportunity to pay tribute to those heroes and make today's generation aware of their bravery.

Acknowledgements

Regards to my parents and families, who raised me to be what I am.

ℵ

Special regards to all my teachers, who made me able to read and write.

ℵ

Special thanks to my best friend Anant,
for supporting me no matter what circumstances were.

I

Chandragupta Maurya

"Life is like a game of cards. The hand you are dealt is determinism; the way you play it is free will." – Jawaharlal Nehru

That was an unfortunate period in world history. The north-western boundaries of the subcontinent were being raided by the forces of Alexander, the king of Macedonia. He was on a mission to conquer the known world. His intense thirst to conquer the whole world spilled the blood of a large number of people. Alexander has had assumed the titles of *Basileus of Macedon, Hegemon of Hellenic League, Autokrator of Greece, Shahanshah of Persia, Pharoh of Egypt,* and *Lord of Asia.* After conquering Egypt, Persia, Western, and Central Asia, he arrived at the doorsteps of the Indian subcontinent. Conquering India, the land of Indus was an important part of Alexander's military campaign. This was due to the cultural, spiritual economic, political, and military influence and might of India, for whom not only Alexander, but hundreds of invaders for thousands of years strived. The fate of India, and probably the world awaited.

Things were also very shaky and unstable in India. The north-western regions of the subcontinent were governed by independent rulers like Ambi *(Omphius)* of *Taxila* and Porus of *Jhelum (Hydaspes).* The central heartland of India and the Gangetic plains were under the authority of the Nanda Empire of *Magadha* under Emperor Dhana Nanda. Contemporary texts suggest that things were not good under the Nandas. Corruption, prejudice, injustice, and misuse of power caused unrest among the people. Acharya Vishnugupta Kautilya, popularly referred to as *Chanakya* writes that Dhana Nanda was an incompetent and luxuriant ruler who was destroying the *Dharma* instead of upholding it.

After defeating the *Aspasioi* and *Assakenoi* sections of the *Kambojas,* and forging an alliance with Ambiraj *(Omphis)* of Taxila, Alexander ensued in a battle with the brave ruler of Jhelum, Porus. At the battle of *Hydaspes, the* forces of the two generals fought, but to the unfortunate of Bharat, Porus lost due to the betrayal of Ambi. Later, Porus was asked by Alexander about how he must be treated? "Like a king treats another king." answered the brave lion of Jhelum. Alexander is said to be deeply impressed by the pride of Porus. Porus was given back his title and territory and was installed as a *Satrap* of Alexander.

Chanakya was worried about the advancing Macedonian forces. According to the popular version, he approached Emperor Dhana Nanda and advised him to unite all Indian kings to fight Alexander. But Dhananand refused to do so in his arrogance. Acharya Chanakya was insulted by Dhananda in the royal court. Chanakya was thrown out by the soldiers. Then Acharya Chanakya, gulping the flames of his humiliation, took a vow that he would end Dhananand's ego and empire. And till this happens, he will not tie his *Shikha* (braid).

Eventually, the army of Alexander mutinied at the *Hyphasis* River (Vyas river) to march ahead into the Gangetic plains. They were afraid of the massive army of Magadha with thousands of Elephants and Chariots. Though Alexander tried to persuade his army, they refused to march any further in India. At last, Alexander agreed to retreat. During their journey back home, they confronted the Indian tribe of *Malhi* (Multan). Alexander sustained injuries in the siege. Alexander eventually died in Babylon at the age of 32 in 323 BC.

There is a debate on the early life of Chandragupta. But he is considered to be born and brought up by a poor *Maurya* clan in *Pataliputra* (Present-day Patna). There is not much clarity about how Chanakya met Chandragupta. According to most popular folklore, when returning from the royal court after being humiliated, Chanakya saw some boys playing in a field. One of them was portraying the emperor, and others were playing the role of subjects. Chandragupta as emperor in the game was giving directions and delivering justice. Seeing the display of such great qualities of a king, Chanakya quickly recognized the potential of Chandragupta. He sought the permission of the boy's clan and mother to take him to *Takshashila*, to train him and hone his skills.

Initially, Chandragupta and Chanakya made north-western India a base for consolidating power. These regions were facing chaos in the post-Macedonian invasion period. This region also lacked political and military leadership. Gradually, he won over the Greco-Macedonian territories. Then they receded into Central India before approaching the doorsteps of the Magadha Empire. But taking down an army as large as Magadha was not a piece of cake. Even Alexander's forces were feared to do so. But Chandragupta had Chankaya on his side. Chanakya, a master strategist and an Acharya of *Rajniti-Shashtra* (Political Science) and *Arth-Shashtra* (Economics) at Takshashila University, and author of *Chanakya Niti and Artha-Shashtra*, was not ready to concede defeat. His pledge and his open *Shikha* were adding ghee to the *Yagya* of revolution in India.

Chanakya realized that enraging a direct battle with Dhanananda will not be wise. Slowly, he started depriving Dhanananda of his key allies and loyalist. He used the secret service to create loopholes and intrude on the Nanda administration. He also fanned the unrest which was prevalent among the masses. Chanakya's political tactics and tricks finally created chaos in

Magadha, leading to a coup. Dhana Nanda was dethroned, and Chandragupta Maurya ascended to the throne of Magadha. Acharya Chanakya became *Maha-Amatya* (Prime Minister) of the empire. The change of power was welcomed by the people, as they saw it as an opportunity to end the oppressive rule of Dhana Nanda.

After consolidating the throne of Magadha, Chandragupta started to expand his empire. Chanakya wanted to make a united Bharat, which is governed by one single government instead of local kings. So that an invader like Alexander could never again look at India with eyes filled with greed. Chandragupta's conquest of north-western regions freed many territories which were under the authority of Greek governers. And these battles may have caused the death of two of Alexander's governors, *Nicanor* and Philip.

After the demise of Alexander, Seleucus I Nicator, one of Alexander's Macedonian generals, established Seleucid Kingdom in 312 BCE. He took authority over Persia and Bactria and established the capital in Babylon. His eastern boundaries faced Chandragupta's empire. Seleucus and Chandragupta ensued a long war, and finally, the Macedonian army had to surrender. *Arachosia (Kandhar), Gedrosia (Baluchistan), and Paropamisadae (Gandhar)* were ceded to the Mauryan empire by Seleucus. Also, the daughter of Seleucus was married off to Chandragupta to establish a matrimonial alliance. Chandragupta gifted 500 war elephants to Seleucus, which led to his victory in the battle of *Ipsus.* Greek scholar *Magasthenes* was appointed as an ambassador in the Mauryan royal court.

After securing the northern boundaries, Chandragupta started to expand his empire southwards. His empire spread beyond the Vindhya range into the Deccan plateau. Two poetic anthologies from the Tamil *Sangam* literature - *Akananuru* and *Purananuru* mention chariots and the army of the Mauryan empire. From the *Hindu Kush* in the north to the *Deccan* in the south, and from *Vanga* in the East to *Gandhara* in the west, this was the mighty Mauryan empire under Chandragupta Maurya. Chandragupta Maurya along with his mentor and *Guru* Chanakya made one of the largest empires to ever exist on the Indian Subcontinent.

After unifying India, Chandragupta under the guidance of Chanakya launched a series of political and economic reforms. The empire was controlled by a structured administration. Chandragupta had a *Mantri-Parishad* (Council of Ministers) headed by Chanakya as *Maha-Amatya* (Prime Minister). The *Samrajya* (Empire) was organized into *Janapadas* (territories), with *Durgas* (Forts) built for the defense of the empire. State operations were funded by the *Kosha* (Imperial Treasury) and alms were regularly given to *Brahmins* and other needy people.

According to Megasthenes, Chandragupta's administrational structure consisted of three parallel branches. One branch managed village affairs, land ownership, irrigation, hunting, forests, wood, and dispute settlement. Another branch looked after city affairs, trade, commerce, infrastructure, markets, and industries. The third branch managed military, training, weapon supply, and soldiers. So what we see is that the Mauryan Empire had a very well-managed and laid-out plan for administration. Better administration not only created a better living for the masses but also ensured the stability of the empire itself.

Infrastructure witnessed a great transformation under the Mauryan rule. irrigation channels, temples, mines, roads, and water reservoirs were built. Greek ambassador Megasthanese noted that Chandragupta built a thousand-mile-long highway connecting the Imperial capital of *Pataliputra* in present-day Bihar to *Takshshila* in present-day Pakistan.

Writer-historian William Durant wrote about Chandragupta Maurya's administration -

> “*"The government made no pretense to democracy and was probably the most efficient that India has ever had. Akbar, the greatest of the Moguls, "had nothing like it, and it may be doubted if any of the ancient Greek cities were better organized."*”

The context of Chandragupta Maurya's death appears in Jain texts such as *Brihakatha Kosha (931 CE) of Harishena, Bhadrabahu Charita (1050 CE) of Ratnanandi, and Munivamsa Bhyudaya (1680 CE). According to Jain texts, Chandragupta abdicated his throne to his son Bindusara around 298 BCE. He moved south to Shravanbelagola* in present-day Karnataka. Chandragupta lived as an ascetic in *Shravanbelagola*. He died in 297 BCE by fasting to death as per the Jain practice of *Sallekhana.*

II

Porus

"No one is wise by birth, for wisdom results from one own's efforts." – T. Krishnamacharya

That was an intriguing period in the known world. A young man from Macedonia had become the ruler of half the world. After conquering the *Balkans, Levant, Syria, Egypt, Assyria, and Babylonia, Alexander* waged war on the powerful *Achaemenid* Empire of *Persia.* After the fall of the Persian empire, Alexander's empire reached the Indian subcontinent. At that time, India was not governed by a single political entity or empire. There were many kingdoms and principalities, ruled by independent kings and lords. The *Nanda Empire* was the most powerful of them all. It had a large army, a prosperous economy, and a vibrant culture. It was ruled by *Dhana Nanda,* an oppressive yet powerful emperor.

Alexander's army was entering the Indian subcontinent from the northwestern frontier areas. That region had a bunch of rulers. *Takshshila, Pauravs, Kambojas,* and *Gandhara* were the primary principalities in the region. During the expedition, Alexander's army defeated Kambojas and Gandhara. These regions were taken into the Macedonian empire. Raja *Ambhi* of *Taxila (Takshshila)* and Raja *Porus* of *Paurava* were sent the offer to bow down to Alexander and continue to rule their kingdoms as *Kshatraps* (Governors) of Alexander.

Ambhi Naresh addressed as *Omphis* in contemporary greek texts, received Alexander with joy. He presented precious presents to Alexander and pledged his loyalty to the Macedonian empire. The rule of Omphis as a *Kshatrap* was confirmed by Alexander. Alexander also provided some Macedonian infantry to Omphis. Ambi wanted to subdue his rivals such as Pauravraj Porus. In Alexander, he saw an opportunity to establish his dominance in north-western India. He hoped that with the backing of Alexander's highly trained infantry and battle techniques, he will overpower all other kings, which stood against him. Ambi is a big clot in Indian history. He compromised the purity and integrity of his pious motherland for the sake of his ambitions. His name was recorded among the major traitors in the history of India.

Porus, born Purushottam (Sanskrit. The best man) was an influential ruler in the north western traits. His kingdom was spread between the river *Hydaspes (Jhelum)* and *Acesines (Chenab).* He was the ruler of the affluent *Paurava* dynasty. The lineage of Pauravs can be traced back to the *Puru* tribe which is mentioned in the *Rigveda.* In many texts, Porus is referred to as *Paurava-Raj Porus.* This indicates that Porus was the leader and king of the Paurava clan.

After gaining the allegiance of *Ambi (Omphis) of Taxila and Abhisara (Abisares) of Abhira,* Alexander was ready to march into the Gangetic plains, to finally conquer India and fulfill his dream. But between Alexander and India, Porus was standing like the great *Himalayas.* Porus had denied accepting the sovereignty of Alexander. Unlike Ambi and Abhisara, he was loyal to his motherland and was willing to fight to the death for it. Porus is among the prolific examples of Hindu kings, who never left their *Raj-Dharma* for personal ambitions or conflict of interests. And this is what the *Sanatana Dharma* (The eternal duty) is all about. Always standing for the good, and against the bad.

At that time Takshshila (Taxila) was an important hub of learning, knowledge, and culture not only in India but for the world. Takshshila University was known to be India's and probably the world's most notable center of learning. Alexander is said to be deeply attracted by the wisdom and exotic culture that he was witnessing in Takshshila. But Porus's decision of not bowing his head down compelled Alexander to engage in a battle with the Pauravas. Alexander along with his army marched to the banks of river Jhelum. The other bank of Jhelum was occupied by Porus and his defense forces.

If you visit the plains of *Punjab* in Pakistan, you would sense that the river *Jhelum* is a deep and fast-moving river. Crossing the river to lead the charge while the opposite bank is occupied by a hostile enemy, the possibility of success in this scenario is very low. Alexander knew this very well. His army needed a safer alternative to cross the river. But this wasn't possible as Porus's army was keeping a close watch on the Macedonian army from the left bank of the river. Alexander needed to trick Porus's diligence to cross the mighty river of *Jhelum.*

Alexander established a camp on the northern bank of the river Jhelum. Each night, Alexander used to move his army up and down along the embankment. This was a bluff to confuse and exhaust the Indian army. Eventually, the Macedonian army found a suitable place for the crossing of *Jhelum.* This crossing was 27 KM (13 miles) upstream of his camp. An uninhabited island was situated mid-stream at this point in the river. Alexander adopted the classic *Pincer Manoeuvre* strategy for the confrontation with the Indian army. Alexander, with a strong contingent, moved upstream towards the marked crossing point. According to the Greek historian *Arrian,* Alexander crossed the river with 6000 foot-soldiers and 5000 horse-riders. Some sources claim it to be even larger.

Craterus, one of Alexander's generals was left to lead at the camp where most of the army was waiting for the command of assault. This was done to create an elusion for Porus that the Macedonian army is still at the camp and hasn't crossed the river yet. Craterus was commanded to attack if Porus faced Alexander with the whole army. And to hold his position if Porus attacked Alexander with a smaller portion of the legion. *Meleager, Attalus, and Gorgias* were commanded to cross the river with their forces from various points on the river. A story goes that a look-alike of Alexander was placed in the royal tent to trick Porus's army.

Alexander landed on the shore by dawn. Showing his tactical instinct, he quickly commanded his contingent to reorganize into a defense gesture. The Companion cavalry was deployed in front of the infantry. The mounted archers served as a defensive guard for cavalry against the Indian elephants. Alexander was afraid that his army will be crushed by the mighty Indian elephants which Porus had. By this time the news of Alexander's arrival on the eastern bank had reached Porus. He was alarmed immediately but we can't say that it was fully unexpected for him. He knew that Alexander was an ambitious and able warrior. The collision of two mighty legions was now inevitable. Alexander was thinking about Porus, and Porus was thinking about Alexander. Two proficient warriors war now ready to test arms and swords with each other. At the end of the battle, one king will get the victory, the other will get eternal glory. The course of history was changing.

Porus did not want to give Alexander the chance to make the first move. Therefore he sent his son with 3000 cavalry and 120 chariots to make a fierce attempt on the Macedonian army. But destiny had already chosen its course. Porus's contingent suffered heavy losses. Porus's son was killed in this futile attempt. Some survivors reached Porus to narrate what just happened. Porus closed his teary eyes and raised his face towards the sky. All that came out of his mouth - Ram!

Without waiting for the additional cavalry to arrive, he advanced 6 miles towards the Indian camp. He waited there till the rest of the infantry crossed *Jhelum.* Greek historian *Arrian of Nicomedia wrote,* "Alexander had no intention of making the fresh enemy troops a present of his own breathless and exhausted men, so he paused before advancing to the attack."

Though there are disagreements on almost every fact regarding the battle of Hydaspes, Historians do agree on Porus's preparations to face the Macedonian army. Porus placed his mighty war elephants afore his infantry. Indian cavalry was deployed in right and left flanks screened by chariots. Porus was astride his elephant right in the middle of his army.

River Jhelum saw the dance of death that day. It was one of the most fierce battles ever fought in India. Alexander relied on the tactics which he learned in Macedonia and mastered in battles in Central India. Alexander used his Companion cavalry to assault the Indian army from the right while the horse archers were thundering on the Indian elephants with arrows. Coenus was assaulting the Indian army from the right while Alexander was attacking from the left. Surrounded by the Macedonians from both sides, sent his elephants to crush the Macedonian phalanx. But Alexander's horse archers were well trained. They launched an attack on Indian elephants with more force. Unfortunately, elephants panicked and revolted, crushing Porus's men. Retreating Indians were attacked by Craterus, who by then had crossed the river.

The battle was over. The Indian army was defeated. Porus was woeful and shocked seeing the fate of his army. But he was still reluctant to admit defeat and surrender. Alexander approached the defeated yet proud king, and asked how he wanted to be treated. "As a King" responded Porus. Greek philosopher Plutarch wrote -

> "*When Porus was taken prisoner, and Alexander asked him how he expected to be used, he answered, "As a king.' For that expression, he said, when the same question was put to him a second time, comprehended everything. And Alexander, accordingly, not only suffered him to govern his own kingdom as satrap under himself but gave him also the additional territory of various independent tribes whom he subdued...*"

Porus did become an ally of Alexander after the battle of Hydaspes. But Alexander was deeply impressed by the courage of Indians. According to Britannica, "The fight on the banks of the Hydaspes River in India was the closest Alexander the Great came to defeat. His feared Companion cavalry was unable to subdue fully the courageous King Porus. Hydaspes marked the limit of Alexander's career of conquest; he died before he could launch another campaign."

III

Harshavardhana

""By plucking her petals, you do not gather the beauty of the flower." – Rabindranath Tagore"

It was the time of the late 6th century. The great *Gupta Empire,* under which India witnessed its "Golden Period", had collapsed. India was again divided into small kingdoms and principalities like *Chachs of Sindh, Pratiharas of* Central India, *Karkotas of Kashmir, Kalchuri of* Eastern India, and *Maitrakas* of Gujarat. In *Deccan, Chalukyas* emerged as the predominant kingdom dominating the plateau and the *Konkan* coast. In the far north, a new dynasty called the *Pushyabhuti* or simply the *Vardhana* dynasty was ruling over a kingdom called *Sthanvishvara.* This place is modern-day Thanesvar in Kurukshetra of Haryana.

Sthanvishvara was ruled by Raja *Prabhakarvardhana* of the Pushyabhuti dynasty. Prabhakarvardhana and his wife *Yashomati* had two sons and one daughter - *Rajyavardhana, Harshvardhana, and Rajyashri.* Princess *Rajyashri* was married to *Grahavarman* of the *Maukhari* dynasty of *Kannauj.* Around this time, the *Hun* tribal people started penetrating the Indian subcontinent through the *Khyber Pass.* They gained control of north-western frontier areas of the subcontinent. Earlier they were promptly defeated by an alliance of Hindu kings *Yashodharman* and *Narsimhagupta.* But after the fall of the Gupta dynasty, some smaller Hun tribes were posing threat to soviergnity of the Vardhana dynasty.

To defeat the invading Huns, Prabhakarvardhana sent his army under the leadership of his two princes - Rajyavardhana and Harshavardhana. The Vardhana duo triumphed in the campaign against the Huns. The invading army was forced to surrender and flee the battleground. After successfully thwarting an invasion attempt, the royal army was preparing to return to the capital city. Just then a messenger arrived at the camp of princes. King Prabhakarvardhana is dead - He told the two prices. Both princes got into tears for their deceased father. A great monarch had passed, and now there was the "*Yaksha Prashna*" which emerges after the death of every king. The question of - Succession.

Both princes arrived at the royal capital. Ministers requested Rajyavardhana to sit on the throne as he was the elder son of Prabhakarvardhana. But Rajyavardhana had something else in mind, he was reluctant to become the king. He suggested that Harsha must be crowned instead. Harsha, a good and loyal brother, insisted on Rajyavardhana's coronation. At last, Rajyavardhana was crowned the king of Sthanvishvara.

About a thousand miles due east from the abode of Pushyabhutis, there was a powerful kingdom called *Gauda* (Present-day Bengal). Raja Shashanka was the ruler of Gauda. He was an ambitious king. He wanted to gain control of the whole of northern India. Defeating the Pushyabhutis was an important task that needed to be accomplished. After the death of Prabhakarvardhana, an inexperienced Rajyavardhana was reigning as king. The Vardhana army had just fought the Huns, so they were exhausted. Shashanka thought that this is the right time to complete his dream.

But there was an obstacle between Shashanka and his dream. It was Raja Grahavrman of Kannauj, the husband of Rajyashri. At the request of his wife, Grahavarman was giving advice and guides the inexperienced prince through his royal duties. To make Rajyavardhana weaker, and to conquer Kannauj it was necessary to remove Grahavarman from the way. Shashanka took a vicious way to defeat him. According to folk legend, Shashanka murdered Grahavarman taking advantage of the crowd during the *Vasant-Utsav* (Spring festival). He captured the capital city of *Kanyakubja.* Rajyashri, the wife of Grahvarman, was taken captive and imprisoned.

Soon the news of the siege of Kannauj reached Rajyavardhana. On hearing that Grahavarman is murdered and his dear sister is taken captive by Shashanka, Rajyavardhana became enraged. He announced that his army will set out for Kannauj to avenge Grahavarman and free Rajyashri. This was the time when everyone in society was ready to fight for upholding *Dharma.* The fate which the royal couple of Kannauj faced was illegitimate according to the Dharma. Due to this notion, a large number of people joined Rajyavardhana's army to fight Shashanka. As he approached Kannauj, Shashanka became suspicious about whether he will be able to win or not. After much thinking, Shashanka sent a treaty proposal to Rajyavardhana.

Rajyavardhana thought that this can stave off a lot of bloodsheds. Great Chinese philosopher Sun Tzu said, "*The wise warrior avoids the battle.*" Rajyavardhana agreed to the peace treaty. It was decided that both kings will meet at a camp. During the meeting, Shashanka treacherously killed Rajyavardhana. Within a year of his father's death, Harsha lost his elder brother too. Now Harshvardhana was the king of Thaneswar at the young age of sixteen. Harsha declared war on the Gauda king Shashanka. He proclaimed to all known kings to either accept his suzerainty or get ready to face battle. After gaining some allies, Harsha marched towards Kannauj to crush Shashanka.

Harshavardhan's life has been well described in the *Harshcharita,* a 7th-century text by Sanskrit scholar-poet *Banabhatta.* According to Harshacharita, Rajyashri escaped the prison of Shashanka and fled to Vindhyas to take refuge. On getting to know this, Harsha hurried to Vindhyas to save his sister. When Harsha arrived, Rajyashri was about to commit suicide. Harsha rescued

Rajyashri just in time.

After making sure Rajyashri's safety and well-being, it was time to punish the insidious Shashanka, who tricked two family members of Harsha into death. Kannauj witnessed a fierce battle between Harshavardhana and Shashanka. Ultimately, Shashanka had to retreat from the battleground after incurring heavy losses. The territory of Kannauj was ceded to Harshavardha, yet Shashanka retained his home kingdom of Gauda and continued to rule it till his death in 625 AD. After Shashanka's death, the kingdom of Gauda was subdued by Harshavardhana.

After the successful siege of Kannauj, Harsha looked out to establish and consolidate an empire. He set out his army in various directions to expand his empire. After some time, he managed to unite almost all of northern India under one empire. This time was the zenith of Pushyabhuti's power. His rigorous conquests made the Chalukyas of the south suspicious of the intentions of Harshavardhana.

They suspected that Harsha will try to invade the Chalukya territories to expand his empire. The tensions grew to the extent of bringing the most powerful northern empire against the most powerful southern empire in the battleground of Narmada valley. Harshavardhana himself led the charge for the Pushyabhutis. The Chalukyas were led by mighty and illustrious king Pulakeshin II who you will read in detail in the tenth chapter. Chinese traveler Hiuen Tsang wrote about the battle :

> “*"Shiladityaraja (Harshavardhana), filled with confidence, marched at the head of his troops to contend with this prince (Pulakeshin); but he was unable to prevail upon or subjugate him".*”

In the confrontation between two pole-like kings of India, finally, Pulakeshin emerged victorious. This was a major setback for Harsha. His army incurred huge losses in the high-pitched battle. A large number of his elephants died in the battle. After the battle, the two mighty kings entered into a peace treaty. This peace treaty established the river Narmada as the Lakshaman-Rekha (Border) between Harshavardhan's and Pulakeshin's empires. Harshavardhana vowed to never again make a move to the south. After the battle with the Chalukyas, Harsha relinquished any further bloodshed and decided to focus on well being of his existing empire. Harshavardhana took the title of "Sakal Uttara Path Nath Maharadhiraja Harshavardhana" meaning - Lord of northern India, King of kings Harshavardhana.

Harshavardhan was a great patron of art and education himself being a scholar. Harsha himself wrote three plays in Sanskrit - Priyadarshika, Ratnavali, and Nagananda. The importance of Nalanda, the great ancient university was at its peak during Harshavardhana's reign. At its zenith, ten thousand students were being taught by two thousand teachers in Nalanda. Vedas, Buddhism, Philosophy, logic, medicine, law, administration, economics, architecture, and astronomy were part of the curriculum. The Nalanda University followed a strict procedure for admission in those days. A rigorous oral examination was conducted by the gatekeepers or the Dwara-Palas. Those who passed were admitted to the university, and most were rejected. The level of literacy of those days can be observed from the fact that the gatekeepers were interviewing the admission-seeking potential candidates. However, this can be assumed that the Dwar-Palas were trained and taught for conducting the interviews.

Harsha was a great devotee of Shiva or Rudra, as he has been addressed in the Vedas, but he patronaged Buddhism. According to his seals, his ancestors were *Surya-Upasak* (Sun-worshippers), and his elder brother Rajyavardhana was a Buddhist. Harsha himself was a *Shaivite Sanatani*. He is described as *Param Maheshvara* (Supreme devotee of Shiva) in his land grant inscriptions. He was tolerant of all faiths and beliefs but worked on propagating Mahayana philosophy. To popularise the *Mahayana* doctrine, Harsha organized a great assembly of scholars in the city of *Kanyakubja*. This assembly was presided over by Chinese scholar

Hiuen Tsang. Harshavardhana started a tradition of organizing a ceremony at *Prayag* every five years. Various scholars and pilgrims used to visit the pious city where the three holy rivers meet.

The grand celebrations used to last 75 days. Deities such as *Buddha, Surya* (Sun), and *Rudra* (Shiva) were worshipped. Valuable presents and clothes were distributed among the visitors. Samrat Harshavardhana performed *Dana* (Charity) during the ceremony. Most of the wealth accumulated in five years was given away to the needy during the Dana ceremony. During one such instance, Harsha gave away even his ornaments and clothes to the poor people. He wore clothes given by his sister Rajyashri.

Harshavardhana ruled for about forty years. His reign ended with his death in 647 AD. Harsha had no heir at the time of his death. He had two sons with his wife Durgavati - *Vagyavardhana* and *Kalyanavardhana.* According to a legend, both princes were murdered before the death of Harshavardhana. With his death, the great empire of the *Pushyabhutis* and the Vardhana dynasty also ended. After Harsha's death, one of his ministers *Arunasva* took the throne for a brief period. Soon Arunasva was succeeded by Raja *Yashovarman.* You will read more about Yashovarman in Chapter 18, *Lalitaditya Muktapida.*

Harshavardhana lost his father, his brother, and his two children. He suffered defeat from the Chalukyas. He suffered the internal strife of his empire. So when we see the life of Harshavardhan, he did not had an easy life. His life was full of challenges, pain, and continuous suffering. But gold ore doesn't become shiny gold till it's put to a certain level of temperature. Likewise, Harsha faced all challenges with a clenched fist and open heart. That's why he will always be remembered as one of the greatest warriors of this land.

IV

Kanishka

> *"Remember, no one is stopping you from lighting a lamp in a dark night." – Harivansh Rai Bacchan*

Kushan dynasty was a powerful empire during the early 1st century. This dynasty was ruled by rulers such as *Kujula Kadphises* and *Vima Kadphises* during different periods. But the kingdom reached its zenith under the reign of *"Kanishka the Great"*. During Kanishka's authority, the Kushan Empire spread from *Bukhara* (now in Uzbekistan) in the west to *Pataliputra* (now in Bihar) in the east and from the *Pamir* mountains (now in Tajikistan) in the north to the Central-Indian plains in the south.

The *Rabtak* inscription was found in 1993 near *Surkh Kotal* in Afghanistan. This large stone inscription dates back to Kanishka's reign in 127 AD. The inscription states *Saket, Kausambi, Ujjain, Kudina, Pataliputra, and Champa* as part of Kanishka's empire. Another stone inscription dated back to the 2nd century was discovered in *Pauni,* south of Narmada. It suggests that Kanishka's empire stretched even further south of the Narmada. In central Asia, Kanishka's empire covered the areas of Balochistan, western Pakistan, Afghanistan, Kyrgyzstan, Tajikistan, Uzbekistan, and Turkmenistan. Having such a vast empire earned Kanishka the title of "great" and thus called Kanishka the Great.

Kanishka's life is rarely known. When we see history, we will observe that most of the great Indian kings had a biography written by a poet. If you want to know about Harshavardhana, there is *Harshacharita* by *Banabhatta.* If you want to read about Lalitaditya Muktapida, there is *Rajtarangini* by *Kalhana.* If you want to know about Raja Dahir, you can read *Chachnama.* The list continues with *Akbarnama* of Abul Fazl and so on. Chronicles play an important role in how the coming generations will see the past rulers. But when we read about Kanishka, there is no such evident work of writing. All the information available is either from later historians, folklores, or the inscriptions found by archaeologists.

Kanishka ascended to the throne in 127 AD succeeding his father *Vima Kadphises.* He established a well-maintained administrative system. Local governments were managed by *Satraps* (Provincial Governors), *Meridareks* (District Officers), and *Strategoi* (Military Governors). These officers were directly appointed by the emperor and were answerable to him.

In ancient times, there was a fashion of kings declaring themselves to be of divine legacy. This was especially prevalent in Europe. Alexander is the most popular example. Kings used to do this to prove their legitimacy and superiority over others. Kanishka also claimed divine legacy by using titles such as "Kings of kings", "Great King", "Emperor" and "Son of Heaven". Kushans deified their kings and dedicated temples to them after death. Kanishka's empire was not only vast but also prosperous. Kushan stronghold in Central India allowed commanding several trade routes and most notably the Silk road.

V

Prithviraj Chauhan

"“Don’t limit a child to your own learning, for he was born in another time.” – Rabindranath Tagore"

"Char haanth chaubis gaj, angul asth praman, taake upar Sultan hai, chuke mat Chauhan" Chand Bardai recited these lines when a blind Rajput king was standing in Ghazni, with bow and arrow in his hands. This was Prithviraj Chauhan. Great Hindu ruler, and arguably the last Hindu ruler to rule over Delhi until it was captured by Hemchandra centuries later. Prithviraj was born in the influential Chauhan or the ‘Chahamana’ clan of Suryavanshi Rajputs. His family ruled over Ajmer in Rajputana.

Prithviraj moved from Gujarat to Ajmer, when his father Someshvara was crowned the Chahamana king after the death of Prithviraja II. Someshvara died in 1177 CE (1234 VS) when Prithviraj was around 11 years old. The last inscription from Someshvara’s reign and the first inscription from Prithviraj’s reign are both dated to this year. Prithviraj, who was a minor at the time, ascended the throne with his mother as the regent. The Hammira Mahakavya claims that Someshvara himself installed Prithviraj on the throne, and then retired to the forest. However, this is doubtful. During his early years as the king, Prithviraj’s mother managed the administration, assisted by a regency council.

Kadambavasa served as the chief minister of the kingdom during this period. He is also known as Kaimasa, Kaimash, or Kaimbasa in the folk legends, which describe him as an able administrator and soldier devoted to the young king. Prithviraj Vijaya states that he was responsible for all the military victories during the early years of his reign. According to two different legends, Kadambavasa was later killed by Prithviraj. The Prithviraj-Raso claims that Prithviraj killed the minister after finding him in the apartment of the king's favorite concubine Karnati. Prithviraj-Prabandha claims that a man named Pratapa-Simha conspired against the minister, and convinced Prithviraj that the minister was responsible for the repeated Muslim invasions. Both these claims appear to be historically inaccurate, as the much more historically reliable Prithviraja Vijaya does not mention any such incident.

Bhuvanaikamalla, the paternal uncle of Prithviraj's mother, was another important minister during this time. According to Prithviraj Vijaya, he was a valiant general who served Prithviraj as Garuda serves Vishnu. The text also states that he was "proficient in the art of subduing nāgas". According to the 15th-century historian Jonaraja, "naga" here refers to elephants. However, Har Bilas Sarda interpreted Naga as the name of a tribe and theorized that Bhuvanaikamalla defeated this tribe.

The 1182–83 CE (1239 VS) Madanpur inscriptions from Prithviraj's reign claim that he "laid to waste" Jejakabhukti (present-day Bundelkhand), which was ruled by the Chandela king Paramardi. Prithviraj's invasion of the Chandela territory is also described in the later folk legends, such as Prithviraj Raso, Paramal Raso, and Alha-Raso. Other texts such as Sarangadhara Paddhati and Prabandha Chintamani also mention Prithviraj's attack on Paramardi. The Kharatara-Gachchha-Pattavali mentions that Prithviraj had embarked upon a Digvijay (conquest of all the regions). This appears to be a reference to the start of Prithviraj's march to Jejakabhukti.

The legendary account of Prithviraj's campaign against the Chandelas goes like this: Prithviraj was returning to Delhi after marrying the daughter of Padamsen, when his contingent was attacked by the "Turkic" forces (Ghurids). His army repulsed the attacks but suffered serious casualties in the process. Amid this chaos, the Chahamana soldiers lost their way and unknowingly encamped in the Chandela capital Mahoba. They killed the Chandela royal gardener for objecting to their presence, which led to a skirmish between the two sides. The Chandela king Paramardi asked his general Udal to attack Prithviraj's camp, but Udal advised against this move. Paramardi's brother-in-law Mahil Parihar ruled modern-day Orai; he harbored ill-will against Paramardi and instigated the king to go ahead with the attack. Prithviraj defeated Udal's contingent and then left for Delhi. Subsequently, unhappy with Mahil's scheming, Udal and his brother Alha left the Chandela court.

They started serving Jaichand, the Gahadavala ruler of Kannauj. Mahil then secretly informed Prithviraj that the Chandela kingdom had become weak in absence of its strongest generals. Prithviraj invaded the Chandela kingdom and besieged Sirsagarh, which was held by Udal's cousin Malkhan. After failing to win over Malkhan through peaceful methods and losing eight generals, Prithviraj captured the fort. The Chandelas then appealed for a truce and used this time to recall Alha and Udal from Kannauj. In support of the Chandelas, Jaichand dispatched an army led by his best generals, including two of his sons. The combined Chandela-Gahadavala army attacked Prithviraj's camp but was defeated. After his victory, Prithviraj sacked Mahoba. He then dispatched his general Chavand Rai to Kalinjar Fort to capture Paramardi. According to the various legends, Paramardi either died or retired shortly after the attack. Prithviraj returned to Delhi after appointing Pajjun Rai as the governor of Mahoba. Later, Paramardi's son recaptured Mahoba.

The exact historicity of this legendary narrative is debatable. The Madanpur inscriptions establish that Prithviraj sacked Mahoba, but historical evidence suggests that his occupation of Chandela territory is either a fabrication by the bards, or did not last long. It is known that Paramardi did not die or retire immediately after the Chauhan victory; in fact, he continued ruling as a sovereign nearly a decade after Prithviraj's death. Cynthia Talbot asserts that Prithviraj only raided Jejakabhukti, and Paramardi regained control of his kingdom soon after his departed Mahoba. Talbot continues that Prithviraj was not able to annex the Chandela territory to his kingdom. Conversely, according to R.B. Singh, it is probable that some part of Chandela territory was annexed by Chahmanas albeit for a short time.

The Kharatara-Gachchha-Pattavali mentions a peace treaty between Prithviraj, and Bhima II, the Chaulukya (Solanki) king of Gujarat. This implies that the two kings were previously at war. This war can be dated to sometime before 1187 CE. The Veraval inscription states that Bhima's prime minister Jagaddeva Pratihara was "the moon to the lotus-like queens of Prithviraja" (a reference to the belief that the moon-rise causes a day-blooming lotus to close its petals). Since Bhima was a minor at the time, it appears that Jagaddeva led the campaign on the Chaulukya side.

The historically unreliable Prithviraj Raso provides some details about the Chahamana-Chaulukya struggle. According to it, both Prithviraj and Bhima wanted to marry Ichchhini, the Paramara princess of Abu. Prithviraj's marriage to her led to a rivalry between the two kings. Historian G. H. Ojha dismisses this legend as fiction because it states that Ichchhini was the daughter of Salakha, while Dharavarsha was the Paramara ruler of Abu at the time. Historian R. B. Singh, on the other hand, believes that Salakha was the head of another Paramara branch at Abu.[26] The Raso also mentions that Prithviraj's uncle Kanhadeva had killed seven sons of Bhima's uncle Sarangadeva. To avenge these murders, Bhima invaded the Chahamana kingdom and killed Prithviraj's father Someshvara, capturing Nagor in the process. Prithviraj re-captured Nagor and defeated and killed Bhima. This is known to be historically false, as the reign of Bhima II lasted nearly half a century after Prithviraj's death. Similarly, historical evidence suggests Bhima II was a child at the time of Someshvara's death, and therefore, could not have killed him.

Despite these discrepancies, there is some evidence of a battle between the Chahamanas and the Chalukyas at Nagor. Two inscriptions found at Charlu village near Bikaner commemorate the death of Mohil soldiers at the battle of Nagor in 1184 CE. The Mohils are a branch of the Chauhans (the Chahamanas), and it the inscriptions may refer to the battle described in Prithviraj Raso.

Sometime before 1187 CE, Jagaddeva Pratihara signed a peace treaty with Prithviraj. According to Kharatara-Gachchha-Pattavali, a chief named Abhayada once sought Jagaddeva's permission to attack and rob the wealthy visitors from Sapadalaksha country (the Chahamana territory). In response, Jagaddeva told Abhayada that he had concluded a treaty with Prithviraj with much difficulty. Jaggadeva then threatened to have Abhayada sewn in a donkey's belly if he harassed the people of Sapadalaksha. Historian Dasharatha Sharma theorizes that the Chahamana-Chaulukya conflict ended with some advantage for Prithviraj, as Jagaddeva appears to have been very anxious to preserve the treaty. According to historians R.C. Majumdar and Satish Chandra, his long drawn-out struggle against Gujarat was unsuccessful and he suffered a reverse against Bhima. Thus, Prithviraj concluded a treaty by 1187 AD.

The Gahadavala kingdom, centered around Kannauj and headed by another powerful king Jayachandra, was located to the east of the Chahamana kingdom. According to a legend mentioned in Prithviraj Raso, Prithviraj eloped with Jayachandra's daughter Samyogita, leading to a rivalry between the two kings.

The legend goes like this: King Jaichand (Jayachandra) of Kannauj decided to conduct a Rajasuya ceremony to proclaim his supremacy. Prithviraj refused to participate in this ceremony, and thus, refused to acknowledge Jaichand as the supreme king. Jaichand's daughter Samyogita fell in love with Prithviraj after hearing about his heroic exploits and declared that she would marry only him. Jaichand arranged a swayamvara (husband-selection) ceremony for his daughter but did not invite Prithviraj. Nevertheless, Prithviraj marched to Kannauj with a hundred warriors and eloped with Samyogita. Two-thirds of his warriors sacrificed their lives in the fight against the Gahadavala army, allowing him to escape to Delhi with Samyogita. In Delhi, Prithviraj became infatuated with his new wife and started spending most of his time with her. He started ignoring the state affairs, which ultimately led to his defeat against Muhammad of Ghor.

This legend is also mentioned in Abu'l-Fazl's Ain-i-Akbari and Chandrashekhara's Surjana-Charita (which names the Gahadavala princess "Kantimati"). Prithviraj Vijaya mentions that Prithviraj fell in love with the incarnation of an apsara Tilottama, although he had never seen this woman and was already married to other women. According to historian Dasharatha Sharma, this is probably a reference to Samyogita. However, this legend is not mentioned in other historical sources such as Prithviraj-Prabandha, Prabandha-Chintamani, Prabandha-Kosha, and Hammira-Mahakavya. The Gahadavala records are also silent about this event, including the supposed Rajasuya performance by Jayachandra.

According to Dasharatha Sharma and R. B. Singh, there might be some historical truth in this legend, as it is mentioned in three different sources. All three sources place the event sometime before Prithviraj's final confrontation with Muhammad of Ghor in 1192 CE.

Prithviraj's predecessors had faced multiple raids from the Muslim dynasties that had captured the north-western areas of the Indian subcontinent by the 12th century. By the late 12th century, the Ghazna-based Ghurid dynasty controlled the territory to the west of the Chahamana kingdom. While Prithviraj was still a child, in 1175 CE, the Ghurid ruler Muhammad of Ghor crossed the Indus River and captured Multan. In 1178 CE, he invaded Gujarat, which was ruled by the Chalukyas (Solankis). During its march to Gujarat, the Ghurid army appears to have passed through the western frontier of the Chahamana kingdom, as evident by the destruction of several temples and sacking of the Bhati-ruled Lodhruva. The Prithviraj Vijaya mentions that the activities of the Ghurid army were like

Rahu to the Chahamana kingdom (in Hindu mythology, Rahu swallows the Sun, causing a solar eclipse). However, it does not mention any military engagement between the two kingdoms. On its way to Gujarat, the Ghurid army besieged the Naddula (Nadol) fort, which was controlled by the Chahamanas of Naddula. Prithviraj's chief minister Kadambavasa advised him not to offer any assistance to the rivals of the Ghurids, and to stay away from this conflict. The Chahamanas did not immediately face a Ghurid invasion, because the Chalukyas of Gujarat defeated Muhammad at the Battle of Kasahrada in 1178 CE, forcing the Ghurids to retreat.

Over the next few years, Muhammad of Ghor consolidated his power in the territory to the west of the Chahamanas, conquering Peshawar, Sindh, and Punjab. He shifted his base from Ghazna to Punjab and made attempts to expand his empire eastwards, which brought him into conflict with Prithviraj.

Prithviraj Vijaya mentions that Muhammad of Ghor sent an ambassador to Prithviraj, but does not provide any details. Hasan Nizami's Taj-ul-Maasir (13th century CE) states that Muhammad sent his chief judge Qiwam-ul Mulk Ruknud Din Hamza to Prithviraj's court. The envoy tried to convince Prithviraj to "abandon belligerence and pursue the path of rectitude", but was unsuccessful. As a result, Muhammad decided to wage a war against Prithviraj.

During 1190–1191 CE, Muhammad of Ghor invaded the Chahamana territory and captured Tabarhindah or Tabar-e-Hind (identified with Bathinda). He placed it under the charge of Zia-ud-din, the Qazi of Tulak, supported by 1200 horsemen. When Prithviraj learned about this, marched towards Tabarhindah with his feudatories, including Govindaraja of Delhi. According to the 16th-century Muslim historian Firishta, his force comprised 200,000 horses and 3,000 elephants.

Muhammad's original plan was to return to his base after conquering Tabarhindah, but when he heard about Prithviraj's march, he decided to put up a fight. He set out with an army and encountered Prithviraj's forces at Tarain. In the ensuing battle,

Prithviraj's army decisively defeated the Ghurids. Muhammad of Ghor was injured and forced to retreat.

Prithviraj did not pursue the retreating Ghurid army, not wanting to invade the hostile territory or misjudge Ghori's ambition. He only besieged the Ghurid garrison at Tabarhindah, which surrendered after 13 months of siege.

Prithviraj seems to have treated the first battle of Tarain as merely a frontier fight. This view is strengthened by the fact that he made little preparations for any future clash with Muhammad of Ghor. According to Prithviraj Raso, during the period preceding his final confrontation with the Ghurids, he neglected the affairs of the state and spent time in merry-making.

Meanwhile, Muhammad of Ghor returned to Ghazni and made preparations to avenge his defeat. According to Tabaqat-i Nasiri, he gathered a well-equipped army of 120,000 select Afghan, Tajik and Turkic horsemen over the next few months. He then marched towards the Chahamana kingdom via Multan and Lahore, aided by Vijayaraja of Jammu.

Prithviraj had been left without any allies as a result of his wars against the neighboring Hindu kings. Nevertheless, he managed to gather a large army to counter the Ghurids. Prithviraj successfully marshaled a sizeable army composed of over 100 Rajput rulers, mainly War elephants, cavalrymen, and foot soldiers. The 16th-century Muslim historian Firishta estimated the strength of Prithviraj's army as 300,000 horses and 3,000 elephants, in addition to a large infantry. This is most likely a gross exaggeration, aimed at emphasizing the scale of the Ghurid victory. Prithviraj wrote a letter to Muhammad of Ghor, promising him no harm if he decided to return to his own country. Muhammad insisted that he needed time to confer with his Ghazna-based brother Ghiyath al-Din. According to Firishta, he agreed to a truce until he received an answer from his brother. However, he planned an attack against the Chahamanas.

According to Jawami ul-Hikayat, Muhammad assigned a few men to keep the fires in his camp burning at night, while he marched off in another direction with the rest of his army. This gave the Chahamanas an impression that the Ghurid army was still encamped, observing the truce. After reaching several miles away, Muhammad formed four divisions, with 10,000 archers each. He kept the rest of his army in reserve. He ordered the four divisions to launch an attack on the Chahamana camp, and then pretend a retreat.

At dawn, the four divisions of the Ghurid army attacked the Chahamana camp, while Prithviraj was still asleep. After a brief fight, the Ghurid divisions pretended to retreat to abyammad's strategy. Prithviraj was thus lured into chasing them, and by the afternoon, the Chahamana army was exhausted as a result of this pursuit. At this point, Muhammad led his reserve force and attacked the Chahamanas, decisively defeating them. According to Taj-ul-Maasir, Prithviraj's camp lost 100,000 men (including Govindaraja of Delhi) in this debacle. Prithviraj himself tried to escape on a horse but was pursued and caught near the Sarasvati fort (possibly modern Sirsa). Subsequently, Muhammad of Ghor captured Ajmer after killing several thousand defenders, enslaved many more, and destroyed the city's temples.

VI

Raja Dahir

"“We can’t change the direction of the wind, but we can adjust the sails.” – Indian proverb"

In the politics of Pakistan, the term *Bab-ul-Islam* is used extensively. The term stands for the "Gateway of Islam". Sindh is referred to as the gateway of Islam into India. On the 10th day of the month of *Ramazan, Yom-e-Bab-Ul-Islam* is celebrated as a public holiday in Pakistan. This day commemorates the successful conquest of Sindh and the first establishment of Islamic rule on Indian soil by Muhammad ibn Qasim in 712 CE. Qasim defeated Raja Dahir Sen at the banks of river *Sindhu* (Indus). But there is hardly any mention of King Dahir and his sacrifice for the sake of this nation.

Maharaja Dahir Sen, commonly referred to as Raja Dahir was the last Hindu ruler of Sindh. Dahir was 3rd king of the *Brahmin* dynasty of Sindh. After the disestablishment of the *Rai* dynasty in 632 CE, a Brahmin named *Chach* founded the *Brahmin* kingdom. Chach ruled as Maharaja for about 40 years between 632 to 671. His rule witnessed the consolidation of Sindh and strong resistance to hostilities from the *Umayyad Caliphate.* Maharaja Chach leads the Sindhi army in successful war campaigns against the Islamic invaders, even killing Umayyad commander *Abdul Aziz. Chach* was succeeded by his brother *Chandar.* His reign lasted for about 8 years until he died in 679. His reign witnessed armed confrontations and later alliance with the *Siharas of Kannauj.*

After the demise of Chandar in 679, Dahir was crowned king of Sindh. Dahir was the eldest ruler of Chach. His rule witnessed a stable administration. But with the throne, he also inherited the conflicts with the Caliphate. Relations were always been tense been the Sindhi kingdom and the Umayyad Caliphate. After the battle of *Karbala* in 680, Raja Dahir extended an offer of asylum to *Imam Hussain* and his followers. However, he was seized at *Karbala* and martyred viciously. But some of his followers eventually got asylum at Raja Dahir's doorsteps.

in 712, Raja Dahir's kingdom was invaded by *Muhammad-ibn-Qasim* on orders of *Al-Hajjaj ibn Yusuf,* the governor of *Basra* province of the Caliphate. The primary reason for the invasion as cited in *Chach Nama* was a pirate raid conducted by the *Meds* tribe off the coast of *Debal.* The raided ship was carrying valuable gifts for the Umayyad Caliph from the king of *Serendib* (Sri Lanka). *Hajjaj* wanted to revenge on the death of his general *Bazil* who was killed fighting Dahir's son *Jaisiah.* He persuaded the Caliph *Al-Walid* to launch a military campaign against the Sindhi ruler.

In this third campaign against the Sindhi kingdom, Hajjaj did extensive planning. The command of the expedition was given to Mohammad-ibn-Qasim, who is said to be 15-17 years old at that time. Al-Hajjaj supervised the campaign from *Kufa.* The army led by Qasim consisted of 6000 Syrian cavalries and *Mawalis* from Iraq. At the border of Sindh, he was joined by an advance guard and 6000 Camel cavalry. Later, reinforcements from the Governor of *Makran* joined the army at *Debal.* Forces from Makran were accompanied by five M*anjaniks* (catapult). Which were instrumental in making fortified walls collapse. Eventually, Qasim's army was joined by *Jats* and *Meds* who wanted to revenge on Dahir.

Debal was the first town assaulted by Qasim's army. The great temple of Debal was destroyed and many were persecuted to death. After winning Debal, the army marched towards the northeast and took towns such as *Nerun* and *Sehwan.* These towns were taken without fighting. War booty and captured slaves were sent to Al-Hajjaj and Caliph. Dahir's army was being prepared on the other side of the river Indus. Qasim crossed the river and was joined by *Thakur* of *Bhatta* and other western jats. At *Aror,* the armies of Dahir and Qasim collided.

Before the battle of Aror, Dahir is said to have given a speech as mentioned in Chahnama -

> “*"I am going to meet the Arabs in open battle, and fight them as best as I can. If I crush them, my kingdom will then be put on a firm footing. But if I am killed honorably, the event will be recorded in the books of Arabia and India and will be talked about by great men. It will be heard by other kings in the world, and it will be said that Raja Dahir of Sindh sacrificed his precious life for the sake of his country, in fighting with the enemy."*”

Dahir's forces fought bravely but were outnumbered by the Umayyad army swelled by Indian traitors. Between the battle, as things were turning worse for the Hindu army, a minister approached Dahir. Minister suggested Dahir to escape and take refuge to any Hindu king in India. To which Dahir replied by saying -

> “*"You should say to them, 'I am a wall between you and the Arab army. If I fall, nothing will stop your destruction at their hands."*”

Then the minister suggested that at least Dahir's family must be sent to a safe place. To which Dahir denied again saying -

> “*"I cannot send away my family to security while the families of my people and nobles remain here."*”

At last, Dahir was killed in the siege. The brave lion of India, who choose death over fleeing from battle, was dead. After his death, his body was decapitated and his head was sent to Al-Hajjaj. Dahir's death was followed by engulfing Sindh into an era of darkness. Qasim's army looted, plundered, and persecuted many Hindus. Hindu women were raped and sent to harems of Umayyad generals and Emirs. Daughters of Raja Dahir were sent to the harem of the Caliph of the Umayyad Caliphate. Dahir lost because his loyalists turned into traitors, and no Hindu king from India was worried to help him. This was a major turning point in history, as many Islamic invaders followed the path scripted by Qasim, to head into Bharat, and loot it of its riches.

Sometime later, a confederacy of Rajput rulers, under the leadership of *Bappa Rawal* drove Umayyad armies out of India. The Umayyads are said to be pushed back to Iran by Bappa Rawal. Rawal established many Rajput posts for defense purposes and one of those, named after him is today known as Rawalpindi.

VII

Lalitaditya Muktapida

"Comfort is no test of truth. Truth is often far from being comfortable." – Swami Vivekananda

Imagine being the youngest prince of a kingdom, with two elder brothers. No chance at the throne, but eventually you not only become the monarch but also rule for 36 years! Or imagine being born in a royal family of Kashmir valley, but you manage to expand your empire to almost entire north India. These are not fables. This is the story of the Emperor of Kashmir, Samrat *Lalitaditya Muktapida.*

Until 625 AD, Kashmir was ruled by the *Gonanda* dynasty. Baladitya was the last ruler of the Gonanda dynasty. Baladitya had no male heir to be his successor to the throne. He married his daughter *Anangalekha* to a *Kayastha* employee named *Durlabhvardhana.* After the death of Baladitya, Durlabhvardhana emerged as the prime contender for the throne as he was the only son-in-law of the deceased king. His coronation as king of Kashmir in 625 AD marked the beginning of the *Karkota* dynasty in Kashmir.

Durlabhvardhana increased the boundaries of his kingdom to present-day *Khyber Pakhtunkhwa* and some regions of Punjab. Xuanzang (commonly known as Hiuen Tsang), a Chinese traveler, visited Kashmir twice during Durlabhvardhana's reign. After Durlabhvardhana, his son *Durlabhaka* was crowned in 662 with the regnal title of Pratapaditya, thus retaining his maternal surname. In 712, Durlabhaka's son *Chandrapida* was crowned with the regnal name of *Vajraditya.* Vajraditya Chandrapida is said to have been assassinated on orders of his brother *Tarapida.* After the death of Chandrapida in 720, Tarapida ascended to the throne. He is described as a tyrannical and oppressive ruler in the chronicles of *Rajatarangini,* the main historical account of the Karkota dynasty. His rule was also short-lived as he died four years later in 725.

In 725, Durlabhaka's youngest son, Muktapida was crowned king of Kashmir. He assumed the regnal title of Lalitaditya as per the tradition. Thus he came to be known as *Lalitaditya Muktapida.* Lalitaditya's accession to the throne happened in very difficult and adverse circumstances. First, he never had expected to be king, as he had two elder brothers, so he did not stand a chance at the throne. Second, Kashmir had lost three kings in less than 15 years. Given the long 50-year reign of Durlabhaka, this was an event of very quick successions. Third, the death of two kings sparked a fire of unrest in the vassal states of Kashmir. There was a high chance of disintegration of the kingdom if not handled properly. Fourth, by that time Arabic and Turkish invaders had grown strong in the west of Kashmir. The kingdom of Sindh had fallen in hands of the Umayyad Caliphate. Also in the east of Kashmir, the Tibetan army was increasing hostilities.

In the words of John Calvin Maxwell, "A leader is one who knows the way, goes the way, and shows the way." Lalitaditya was certainly a leader which proved this statement. With his wise judgment and courage, he not only consolidated his kingdom of Kashmir but expanded his empire beyond the Kashmiri valley. He came to be counted among those kings who can be called emperors by historians.

Sanjay Sonwani in his book "Emperor of Kashmir Lalitaditya - The Great" writes - "The history of Lalitaditya is very significant for the Indian subcontinent. It throws light on the connection India had with the rest of the world and the nature of her political and social relationships with it. Moreover, we come to know that this valiant king did not just keep the then superpowers China and Tibet at bay through his diplomacy and his military power, but he also extended the boundaries of his Kashmiri Empire to the north of the Hindukush and Pamir ranges."

Lalitaditya started his *Digvijaya* with the conquest of northwestern provinces. Lalitadiya conquered Punjab, Afghanistan, and parts of central Asian highlands before setting foot in Gangetic plains and central India. Lalitaditya's conquest of Afghanistan is assumed to be before 730 AD. Before Lalitaditya, Afghanistan was controlled by *Turkic Shahi,* which were politically influenced by Chinese rulers since the fall of the *Sasanian Empire.* After Lalitaditya's conquest, the control of *Hindu Shahis* was established. *Lalitaditya* defeated Islamic invader *Mummuni* thrice. Umayyad armies were not able to move ahead of Multan because Lalitaditya's empire was powerful enough to beat the Chaliphite forces.

After securing the northern front, Lalitaditya attacked the kingdom of *Kanyakubja (Kannauj).* There was a fierce battle between Lalitaditya and Kannauj's king Yashovarman. After a long battle, and a lot of bloodsheds, both kings agreed to sign a peace treaty to end the war. Yashovarman drafted a peace treaty outlining major agreements between both kings. The treaty was titled "The treaty of King Yashovarman and King Lalitaditya." This enraged Lalitadiya's minister *Mitrasharman.* He insisted that the name of Lalitaditya must appear first in the title of the treaty as Muktapida was the graeter ruler and had the upper hand in the engagement with Kannauj. King Lalitaditya agreed to his minister's view and called off all peace negotiations. The war was resumed between both armies and finally, lead to the defeat of Yashovarman. Yashovarman's kingdom came under the authority of Lalitaditya.

Lalitaditya's army marched eastwards from *Kanyakubja* along the length of the river Ganges. He conquered the kingdoms of *Kalinga (Odisha) and Gauda (Bengal).* From the eastern shores, Lalitadiya marched towards Deccan. At that time, Karnatka was under the control of Queen *Ratta,* who is described to be as powerful as goddess *Vindhyavasini (a form of Durga).* Even being so powerful, *Maharani Ratta* surrendered to Lalitaditya and accepted his suzerainty. The reason for this is considered to be a family feud in which the legitimacy of Ratta on the throne was questioned. Rattawanted to secure his power with help of an influential king like Muktapida.

After concluding the campaign in the south, Lalitaditya's army marched north crossing *Konkan, Avantika (Ujjain), Chittaurgarh, Marwar, and Thaneshwar. Lalitaditya* is said to have conquered *Kathiawar* between 740 and 746 AD. Lalitaditya was forced to return to Kashmir due to the Tibetan invasion in 747. Tibetan king *Me Agtsom* invaded *Kashmir.* After returning to the valley, Lalitaditya strongly repulsed the Tibetan army. Lalitaditya's army even moved forward to take Tibetan territories such as the *Tarim* basin and towns in *Taklamakan* and *Gobi* deserts as described as the "Sea of sand". After a long expedition, Lalitaditya Muktapida managed to build an empire swaying from *Pir-Panjal to Bengal.*

Lalitaditya was not only a great warrior, but he was a great ruler too. He made arrangements to enhance agriculture by building a water wheels system in *Chakradhara.* This arrangement ensured the irrigation of fields from the water of river *Vitasta.* Great architectural marvels were achieved during Lalitaditya's reign. Cities of *Sunishchitapura, Darpitapura, Phalapura, Parnotsa, Lokpunyapur, and Parihaspura* were constructed by Lalitaditya Muktapida. Parihaspura was constructed north of Shri-Nagar and served as the capital of Lalitaditya along with Shri-Nagar. Great temples and Buddhists were also built by Lalitaditya. Most notably, the Martand Sun temple was built by Lalitaditya Muktapida. Unfortunately, that temple was later destroyed by Muslim invaders in the name of *Jihad.* The Martand temple was labeled as "*Shaitan ki Gufa*"(cave of Satan) to create a sense of inferiority and defeat in minds of Hindus.

After reigning for 36 years, Lalitaditya died in 760 AD. He was succeeded by his son *Kuvaladitya.* Youngest prince of Kashmir, who ascended to the throne after the death of his father and two brothers. A young man from Kashmir, the land of *Kashyap Muni.* A king who dreamed of conquering India. An emperor who *Ajay (invincible)* to *Turks, Arabs, and Tibetans.* The true icon of Kashmir, was the great emperor, *Samrat Lalitaditya Mukatpida.*

VIII

Maharana Pratap

"Blaming your faults on your nature does not change the nature of your faults." – Indian proverb

Maharana Pratap is arguably the most significant and illustrious Rajput king of the medieval period. He was born on 9 May 1540 at Kumbhalgarh fort. His father was *Maharana Udai Singh II* of *Mewar.* His mother was *Maharani Jaiwanta Bai.* By the time of Udai Singh's reign, most of the Rajput rulers joined hands with Akbar and accepted Mughal Empire's sovereignty. But the Rajputs of Mewar were still independent with pride. This proudly high head of Mewar was not pleasing to *Akbar.* He was constantly striving to either befriend or destroy Mewar. This was due to his fear that Rajputs were very brave people, and in future the can pose threat to his empire, as once *Hemchandra* to his father *Humayun.*

These tensions between the Rajputs and Mughals resulted in the Siege of Chittorgarh in 1567. Mughal forces entered the fortress and raged a bloody battle. After gaining control of Chittorgarh, Akbar ordered a mass massacre of non-combatants inside the fort. This resulted in the death of 30,000 innocent people who had no means of self-defense. Rajput women of Chittorgarh committed *Johar* to save their honour.

This incident This incident left a wound in the heart of Maharana Pratap. He saw his family, friends, uncles, and brothers dying. He saw his aunts and sisters embracing the shawl of fire to defend their honour. In 1572, Pratap ascended to the throne of Mewar after the death of his father. He vowed to never submit to the Mughals and defend the independence of his motherland till the last breath. Even after getting the leverage after the siege of Chittor, Akbar was still insecure about Rana Pratap. He was suspicious that he may forge unity amongst Hindu Rajputi kingdoms and challenge Akbar's authority. Therefore cunningly he deputed Raja Man Singh of Amer to deal with Pratap.

Man Singh was himself a Hindu Rajput from the kingdom of Amer. As part of the *Navaratna* of Akbar, Man Singh was among the most illustrated figures of Akbar's royal court. Man Singh first tried to convince Pratap through conversation. He visited Pratap's palace to meet him. When the meals were served, Pratap refused to eat with Man Singh as according to him the latter had sold his motherland to Mughals in exchange for a wealthy and comfortable life.

Man Singh was enraged by such treatment. He left the Mewar for the imperial Mughal Capital. Man Singh informed that Maharana Pratap will not accept Mughal sovereignty. Now the war was inevitable. Armies of Maharana Pratap and Raja Man Singh collided at the narrow mountain pass of Haldighati. Mewari soldiers were heavily outnumbered by the Mughal army. Mughals used heavy gunpowder and cannons which the Mewar lacked. Mughals emerged victorious in the battle of Haldighati. Rajput soldiers were killed by fellow Rajput soldiers. This is a classic example of why India was enslaved at different intervals of time. Both Rana Pratap and Man Singh were Rajputs but were still fighting with each other. While Akbar was sitting calmly in his royal palace. 'Divide and Rule' was introduced in India much before the Brits came.

Though the battle was won, the Mughal army was not able to capture Rana Pratap. Therefore this victory was more or less futile for the Mughals. Maharana escaped to the jungles of Aravalli. The next few years of his life were the hardest for him. Like Shri Rama, he had to spend an exile in the forest, despite being a prince. According to the folk legends, he ate *Rotis* made of grass and vowed not to sleep on a comfortable bed till his motherland is not free from invaders.

As time passed, he slowly consolidated his position in Mewar by securing forts one by one. By 1583 he had successfully retained most of his kingdom, but Chittor Durg still had the Mughal flag. Unfortunately, he was never able to return his beloved Chittor in his lifetime. He ruled as a proud king till his death in 1597 at the age of 56. He was succeeded by his eldest son Amar Singh, who ultimately joined the Mughal Empire.

IX

Raja Raja Chola

> "*"What we possess is temporary, but what we become is permanent." – Devdutt Pattanaik*"

Rajaraja's original name was Arulmoḷi (also transliterated as Arulmozhi) Varman, literally "blessed tongued". He was a son of the Chola king Parantaka II (alias Sundara) and queen Vanavan Mahadevi. He had an elder brother – Aditya II, and an elder sister – Kundavai. As he had an elder brother, he was certainly not meant to be the Chola king in the future. But history adopts its course. Destiny wanted Raja as king, so it happened. This is the story of the king, who was not meant to be king.

Rajaraja's elder brother died before him, and after the death of Uttama (his uncle), Rajaraja ascended the throne in June–July 985. Known as Arumoḷi Varman until this point, he adopted the name Rajaraja, which literally means "King among Kings". He also called himself Shivapada Shekhara, literally, "the one who places his crown at the feet of Shiva". This suggests that Raja Raja favored the Nayanars in the Bhakti tussle between the Alvars and Nayanars.

Rajaraja inherited a kingdom whose boundaries were limited to the traditional Chola territory centered around the Thanjavur-Tiruchirappalli region.[1] At the time of his ascension, the Chola kingdom was relatively small and was still recovering from the Rashtrakuta invasions in the preceding years. Rajaraja turned it into an efficiently-administered empire that possessed a powerful army and a strong navy. This displays his leadership skills. During his reign, the northern kingdom of Vengi became a Chola protectorate, and the Chola influence on the eastern coast extended as far as Kalinga in the north.

A number of regiments are mentioned in the Thanjavur inscriptions. These regiments were divided into elephant troops, cavalry, and infantry and each of these regiments had its own autonomy and were free to endow benefactions or build temples.

Rajaraja's inscriptions start to appear in the Kanyakumari district in the 990s and in the Trivandrum district in the early 1000s. The Chola subjugation of Malayali regions (Present day Kerala) can be dated to the early years of the 11th century. The *Senur* inscription (1005 CE) of Rajaraja states that he destroyed the Pandya capital Madurai; conquered the "haughty kings" of Kollam (Venad), Kolla-desham (Mushika), and Kodungallur (the Chera Perumal).

After defeating the Pandyas, Rajaraja adopted the title Pandya Kulashani ("Thunderbolt to the Race of the Pandyas"), and the Pandya country came to be known as "Rajaraja Mandalam" or "Rajaraja Pandinadu". While describing the Rajaraja's campaign in trisanku kastha (the south), the Thiruvalangadu Grant of Rajendra I states that he seized certain royal Amarabhujanga. Identification of this prince (either a Pandya prince or a general of the Pandya king or a Kongu Chera prince) remains unresolved. Kongu Desa Rajakkal, a chronicle of the Kongu Nadu region, suggests that this general later shifted his allegiance to Rajaraja, and performed the Chola king's kanakabhisheka ceremony.

After consolidating his rule in the south, Rajaraja assumed the title Mummudi Chola ("the Chola who Wears Three Crowns"), a reference to his control over the three ancient Tamil countries of the Cholas, the Pandyas, and the Cheras.

In 993, Rajaraja invaded Sri Lanka. Lanka is described as Ila-Mandalam by the Cholas. This invasion most probably happened during the reign of Mahinda V of Anuradhapura, who according to the Chulavamsa chronicle, had fled to Rohana (Ruhuna) in south-eastern Sri Lanka because of a military uprising.[26] The Chola army sacked Anuradhapura, and captured the northern half of Sri Lanka. The Cholas established a provincial capital at the military outpost of Polonnaruwa, naming it Jananatha Mangalam after the title of Rajaraja. The Chola official Tali Kumaran erected a Shiva temple called Rajarajeshvara ("Lord of Rajaraja") in the town of Mahatittha (modern Mantota), which was renamed Rajaraja-pura.

Comparing Rajaraja's campaign to the invasion of Lanka by the legendary hero Rama, the Thiruvalangadu Plates states:

> “*"Rama built with the aid of monkeys, a causeway across the sea, and then with great difficulties defeated the king of Lanka by means of sharp-edged arrows. But Rama was excelled by this king whose powerful army crossed the ocean by ships and burnt up the king of Lanka." — Thiruvalangadu Copper Plates*”

In 1017, Rajaraja's son Rajendra I completed the Chola conquest of Sri Lanka. The Cholas controlled Sri Lanka until 1070 when Vijayabahu I defeated and expelled them.

> “*"A naval campaign led to the conquest of the Maldive Islands, the Malabar Coast, and northern Sri Lanka, all of which were essential to the Chola control over trade with Southeast Asia and with Arabia and eastern Africa. These were the transit areas, ports of call for the Arab traders and ships to Southeast Asia and China, which were the source of the valuable spices sold at a high profit to Europe."*
>
> *— Romila Thapar, (From Encyclopaedia Britannica)*”

One of the last conquests of Rajaraja was the naval conquest of the islands of Maldives. The naval campaign was a demonstration of the Chola naval power in the Indian Ocean. The Cholas controlled the area around of Bay of Bengal with Nagapattinam as the main port. The Chola Navy also played a major role in the invasion of Sri Lanka. The success of Rajaraja allowed his son Rajendra Chola to lead the Chola invasion of Srivijaya, carrying out naval raids in South-East Asia and briefly occupying Kadaram.

X

Krishnadevaraya

"To keep your mind and nature cleansed of impurities, make a hut for your critics in your backyard and keep them close." – Kabir

We all are familiar with the tales of Krishnadevaraya and Tenali Raman. Respect for Krishnadevaraya is enormous within the Indian folk culture. Krishnadevaraya was the third emperor of the Tuluva dynasty which ruled over the Vijayanagara Empire. His empire was very rich and powerful. Under Krishnadevaraya, Vijayanagara witnessed its golden period.

The might of Krishnadevaraya can be assumed by seeing the titles assumed by him in different periods - Karnatakaratna Simhasanadeeshwara ("Lord of the Jewelled Throne of Karnataka"), Yavana Rajya Pratistapanacharya ("Establishment of the King to Bahmani Throne"), Kannada Rajya Rama Ramana ("Lord of the Kannada Empire), Andhra Bhoja ("Scholar of Andhra"), Gaubrahmana Pratipalaka ("Protector of Brahmins and Cows") and Mooru Rayara Ganda ("Lord of Three Kings").

He became the dominant ruler of the peninsula by defeating the sultans of Bijapur, Golconda, the Bahmani Sultanate, and the *Gajapatis* of Odisha, and was one of the most powerful Hindu rulers in India. When the Timurid king Babur invaded north India, he acknowledged Krishnadevaraya as the greatest Hindu king of India along with Rana Sanga, the king of Chittor. The Portuguese travelers Domingo Paes and Duarte Barbosa visited the Vijayanagara Empire during his reign, and their travelogues indicate that the king was not only an able administrator but also an excellent general, leading from the front in battle and even attending to the wounded.

Krishnadevaraya's father was Tuluva Narasa Nayaka. Nayaka was an army commander under Saluva Narasimha Deva Raya, who later took control to prevent the disintegration of the empire and established the Tuluva dynasty of the Vijayanagara Empire. He was married to Srirangapatna's princess Tirumala Devi and Chinna Devi. He was father of Tirumalamba (from Tirumala Devi), Vengalamba (from Chinna Devi) and Tirumala Raya (from Tirumala Devi). His daughters were married to Prince Aliya Rama Raya of Vijayanagara and his brother Prince Tirumala Deva Raya.

The raid and plunder of Vijayanagar towns and villages by the Deccan sultans came to an end during the Raya's rule. In 1509, Krishnadevaraya's armies clashed with them and Sultan Mahmud was severely injured and defeated. Yusuf Adil Shah was killed and the Raichur Doab was annexed. Taking advantage of the victory, the Raya reunited Bidar, Gulbarga, and Bijapur into Vijayanagar and earned the title "establisher of the Yavana kingdom".

The Gajapatis of Odisha ruled a vast land comprising Bengal, the Andhra region, and Odisha. Krishna Deva Raya's success at Ummatur provided the necessary impetus to carry his campaign into The coastal Andhra region which was in control of the Gajapati Raja Prataparudra Deva. The Vijayanagar army laid siege to the Udayagiri fort in 1512. The campaign lasted for a year before the Gajapati army disintegrated due to starvation. Krishna Deva Raya offered prayers at Tirupati thereafter, along with his wives Tirumala Devi and Chinnama Devi. The Gajapati army was then met at Kondaveedu, where the armies of Vijayanagara, after establishing a siege for a few months, began to retreat due to heavy casualties. Then Timmarusu discovered a secret entrance to the unguarded eastern gate of the fort and launched a night attack that culminated with the capture of the fort and the imprisonment of Prince Virabhadra, the son of Prataparudra Deva. Vasireddy Mallikharjuna Nayak took over as governor of Kondaveedu thereafter.

Krishnadevaraya planned an invasion of Kalinga, but Prataparudra learned of this plan and formulated his own plan to defeat Krishandevaraya and the Vijayanagara Empire at the fort of Kalinganagar. But the wily Timmarusu discovered Prataparudra's plan by bribing a Telugu deserter from the service of Prataparudra. When the Vijayanagara Empire did invade, Prataprudra was driven to Cuttack, the capital of the Gajapati Kingdom. Prataparudra eventually surrendered to the Vijayanagara Empire, and gave his daughter, Princess Jaganmohini, in marriage to Sri Krishnadevaraya. Krishandevaraya returned all the lands that the Vijayanagara Empire had captured north of the Krishna River; this made the Krishna river the boundary between the Vijayanagar and Gajapati Kingdoms.

Krishnadevaraya established friendly relations with the Portuguese in Goa in 1510. The Emperor obtained guns and Arabian horses from the Portuguese merchants. He also utilized Portuguese expertise to improve the water supply to Vijayanagara City.

The highlight of his conquests occurred on 19 May 1520 when he secured Raichur Fort from Ismail Adil Shah after a difficult siege in which 16,000 Vijayanagara soldiers were killed. The exploits of the military commander, Pemmasani Ramalinga Nayudu of the Pemmasani Nayaks, during the Battle of Raichur were distinguished and lauded by Krishnadevaraya. It is said that 700,000-foot soldiers, 32,600 cavalry, and 550 elephants were used.

Krishnadevaraya was strict towards the Bahmani Generals of Raichur. Many Bahmani generals lost their lands. The other Muslim kings sent envoys to the emperor on hearing of his success. The king conveyed that if Adil Shah would come to him, do obeisance, and kiss his foot, his lands would be restored to him. The submission never took place. Krishnadevaraya then led his army as far north as Bijapur and occupied it. He imprisoned three sons of a former king of the Bahmani dynasty, who had been held captive by the Adil Shah and he proclaimed the eldest as king of the Deccan. Finally, in his last battle, he razed to the ground the fortress of Gulburga, the early capital of the Bahmani sultanate.

In 1524, Krishnadevaraya made his son Tirumala Raya the Yuvaraja (crown prince). The prince did not survive for long: he was poisoned. Suspecting Timmarusu, Krishna Deva Raya had him blinded. At the same time, Krishnadevaraya was preparing for an attack on Belgaum, which was in Adil Shah's possession. Around this time, Krishnadevaraya fell ill and eventually died in 1529, succeeded by his brother, Achyuta Deva Raya.

XI

Peshwa Bajirao

"Man needs his difficulties because they are necessary to enjoy success." – A.P.J. Abdul Kalam

Baji Rao was born into a Bhat Family in Sinnar, near Nashik. His father was Balaji Vishwanath, the Peshwa of Shahu I. Baji Rao spent his childhood in Saswad. Baji Rao was inspired by the lives of Shivaji, Ramchandra Pant Amatya, and Santaji Ghorpade.

He was trained as a diplomat and a warrior. Being born in a Brahmin family, his education included reading, writing, and learning Sanskrit. But he did not remain stuck to book knowledge only. Baji Rao displayed a passion for the military at an early age and often accompanied his father on military campaigns. He was with his father when his father was imprisoned by Damaji Thorat before being released for ransom. Baji Rao had been on the expedition to Delhi in 1719 with his father and was convinced that the Mughal Empire was disintegrating and unable to resist northward Maratha expansion.

Baji Rao was appointed Peshwa, succeeding his father, by Shahu on 17 April 1720. By the time of his appointment, the Mughal emperor Muhammad Shah had upheld Maratha's claims to the territories held by Shivaji at his death. A treaty gave the Marathas the right to collect taxes (Chauth) in the Deccan's six provinces. Baji Rao convinced Shahu that the Maratha Empire had to go on the offensive against its enemies to defend itself. He believed that the Mughal Empire was in decline, and wanted to take advantage of the situation with aggressive expansion into North India. Baji Rao compared the Mughals' declining fortune to a tree that, if attacked at its roots, would collapse. He said:

> *"Let us strike at the trunk of the withering tree and the branches will fall off themselves. Listen but to my counsel and I shall plant the Maratha flag on the walls of Attock."*

As a new Peshwa, however, he faced several challenges. His appointment at a young age evoked jealousy from senior officials such as Naro Ram Mantri, Anant Ram Sumant, Shripatrao Pant Pratinidhi, Khanderao Dabhade and Kanhoji Bhosle. Baji Rao promoted young men like himself, such as Malhar Rao Holkar, Ranoji Shinde, the Pawar brothers and Fateh Singh Bhosle, as commanders; these men did not belong to families who were hereditary aristocrats. Also, the Purandare family who were the close associates of the Bhat Peshwa family, largely contributed toBaji Rao's success.

The Mughal viceroy of the Deccan, Nizam-ul-Mulk Asaf Jah I, had created a de facto autonomous kingdom in the region. He challenged Shahu's right to collect taxes on the pretext that he did not know whether Shahu or his cousin, Sambhaji II of Kolhapur, was the rightful heir to the Maratha throne. The Marathas needed to assert their rights over the nobles of newly acquired territories in Malwa and Gujarat. Several nominally-Maratha areas were not actually under the Peshwa's control; for example, the Siddis controlled the Janjira fort. All these circumstances were the responsibility of Bajirao to solve.

On 4 January 1721, Baji Rao met Nizam-ul-Mulk Asaf Jah I at Chikhalthana to resolve their disputes. However, the Nizam refused to recognize the Maratha's right to collect taxes from the Deccan provinces. He was made vizier of the Mughal Empire in 1721 by emperor Muhammad Shah, alarmed at his increasing power, and transferred him from the Deccan to Awadh in 1723. The Nizam rebelled against the order, resigned as vizier, and marched towards the Deccan. The emperor sent an army against him, which the Nizam defeated at the Battle of Sakhar-kheda; this forced the emperor to recognize him as viceroy of the Deccan. The Marathas, led by Baji Rao, helped the Nizam win this battle. For his valor, Baji Rao was honored with a robe, a 7,000-man mansabdari, an elephant, and a jewel. After the battle, the Nizam tried to appease the Maratha Chhatrapati Shahu and the Mughal emperor; in reality, however, he wanted to carve out a sovereign kingdom and considered the Marathas his rivals in the Deccan.

In 1725, the Nizam sent an army to clear Maratha revenue collectors from the Carnatic region (Peninsular South-India). The Marathas dispatched a force under Fateh Singh Bhosle to counter him; Baji Rao accompanied Bhosle but did not command the army. The Marathas were forced to retreat; they launched a second campaign after the monsoon season, but again were unable to prevent the Nizam from ousting the Maratha collectors.

In the Deccan, Sambhaji II of Kolhapur State had become a rival claimant to the title of Maratha King. The Nizam took advantage of the internal dispute, refusing to pay the chauth because it was unclear who was the real Chhatrapati (Shahu or Sambhaji II) and offering to arbitrate. Shripatrao Pant Pratinidhi advised Shahu to begin negotiations and agree to arbitration. Sambhaji II was supported by Chandrasen Jadhav, who had fought Baji Rao's father a decade earlier. But Baji Rao convinced Shahu to refuse the Nizam's offer and launch an assault.

The Nizam invaded Pune, where he installed Sambhaji II as the King. He then marched out of the city, leaving behind a contingent headed by Fazal Beg. The Nizam plundered Loni, Pargaon, Patas, Supa, and Baramati, using his artillery. On 27 August 1727, Baji Rao began a retaliatory guerilla attack on the Nizam with his trusted lieutenants Malhar Rao Holkar, Ranoji Shinde, and the Pawar brothers. He began to destroy the towns held by the Nizam; leaving Pune, he crossed the Godavari River near Puntamba and plundered Jalna and Sindkhed. Baji Rao destroyed Berar, Mahur, Mangrulpir, and Washim before turning north-west to Khandesh. He crossed the Tapi River at Kokarmunda and entered eastern Gujarat, reaching Chota Udaipur in January 1728.

After hearing that the Nizam had returned to Pune, Baji Rao feinted toward Burhanpur; he thought that after hearing about the threat to the strategically-important Burhanpur, the Nizam would try to save it. Baji Rao did not enter Burhanpur, however, arriving at Betawad in Khandesh on 14 February 1728. When the Nizam heard that his northern territories had been devastated by Baji Rao, he left Pune and marched towards the Godavari to meet Baji Rao on an open plain where his artillery would be effective. The Nizam went on ahead of his artillery; on 25 February 1728, the armies of Baji Rao and the Nizam faced each other at Palkhed, a town about 30 miles (48 km) west of Aurangabad. The Nizam was quickly surrounded by Maratha forces and trapped, his lines of supply and communication were cut. He was forced to make peace; he signed the Treaty of Mungi Shevgaon on 6 March, recognising Shahu as the King and the Maratha right to collect taxes in the Deccan.

> “*"This campaign gives a classic example of what the predatory horse, when led by a genius, could achieve in the age of light artillery."*
>
> *- Military History of India by Jadunath Sarkar*”

In 1723, Baji Rao organized an expedition to southern Malwa. Maratha chiefs, including Ranoji Shinde, Malhar Rao Holkar, Udaji Rao Pawar, Tukoji Rao Pawar, and Jivaji Rao Pawar, had collected Chauth from several parts of the province. (Later, these chiefs carved out their own kingdoms: Gwalior, Indore, Dhar, and Dewas). To counter Maratha's influence, the Mughal emperor had appointed Girdhar Bahadur governor of Malwa.

After defeating the Nizam, Baji Rao again turned his attention to Malwa. He consigned a large army in October 1728 to his younger brother, Chimaji Appa, and was aided by his trusted generals Udaji Pawar and Malhar Rao Holkar. The Maratha force reached the southern bank of the Narmada River on 24 November 1728. The following day, they crossed the river and encamped near Dharampuri. Marching rapidly northwards, they crossed the ghat near Mandu and halted at Nalchha on 27 November. The Mughal forces, led by Girdhar Bahadur and his cousin Daya Bahadur, hastily prepared to oppose them on hearing that the Maratha army had begun to climb the ghats. Girdhar Bahadur believed that the Marathas, thinking that the pass near the Mandu fort was well guarded, would climb the ghat near Amjhera; he and his army marched to Amjhera and took up a strong position there.

Since the Marathas did not appear there, he suspected that they climbed near the Mandu fort and set out for Dhar on 29 November 1728. Girdhar Bahadur found Maratha horsemen coming toward him. In the 29 November Battle of Amjhera, Chimaji's army defeated the Mughals; Girdhar Bahadur and Daya Bahadur were killed. The Mughal forces fled, and their camp was plundered; eighteen elephants, horses, drums and other loot were taken by the Marathas. News of the victory reached the ears of Peshwa, who was visiting Chhatrasal. Chimaji marched towards Ujjain, but had to retreat due to a lack of supplies. By February 1729, Maratha forces had reached present-day Rajasthan.

In Bundelkhand, Chhatrasal rebelled against the Mughal Empire and established an independent kingdom. In December 1728, a Mughal force led by Muhammad Khan Bangash attacked him and besieged his fort and family. Although Chhatrasal repeatedly sought Baji Rao's assistance, he was busy in Malwa at the time. In his letter to Baji Rao, Chhatrasal wrote the following words:

> "*Know you, that I am in the same sad plight in which the famous elephant was when caught by the crocodile. My valiant race is on point of extinction. Come and save my*

honour, O Baji Rao."

In March 1729, the Peshwa responded to Chhatrasal's request and marched towards Bundelkhand with 25,000 horsemen and his lieutenants Pilaji Jadhav, Tukoji Pawar, Naro Shankar, and Davalji Somwanshi. Chhatrasal escaped capture and joined the Maratha force, increasing it to 70,000 men. After marching to Jaitpur, Baji Rao's forces surrounded Bangash and cut his supply and communication lines. Bangash launched a counterattack against Baji Rao, but could not pierce his defenses. Qaim Khan, son of Muhammad Khan Bangash, learned of his father's predicament and approached with fresh troops. His army was attacked by Baji Rao's forces, and he was defeated. Bangash was later forced to leave, signing an agreement that "he would never attack Bundelkhand again". Chhatrasal's position as ruler of Bundelkhand was restored. He granted a large jagir to Baji Rao and gave him his daughter Mastani in marriage.

After consolidating Maratha's influence in central India, Baji Rao decided to assert the Maratha right to collect taxes from the wealthy province of Gujarat and sent a Maratha force under Chimaji Appa there in 1730. Sarbuland Khan, the province's Mughal governor, ceded the right to collect Chauth to the Marathas. He was soon replaced by Abhay Singh, who also recognized the Maratha right to collect taxes. This irked Shahu's Senapati (commander-in-chief), Trimbak Rao Dabhade, whose ancestors had raided Gujarat several times and asserted their right to collect taxes from the province. Annoyed at Baji Rao's control of what he considered his family's sphere of influence, he rebelled against the Peshwa. Two other Maratha nobles from Gujarat, Damaji Rao Gaekwad and Kadam Bande, also sided with Dabhade.

After Girdhar Bahadur's defeat in 1728, the Mughal emperor appointed Jai Singh II to subdue the Marathas. Jai Singh recommended a peaceful agreement; the emperor disagreed, replacing him with Muhammad Khan Bangash. Bangash formed an alliance with the Nizam, Trimbak Rao and Sambhaji II. Baji Rao learned that Dabhade and Gaikwad had made preparations for an open fight on the plain of Dabhoi with a force of 40 thousand, while Baji Rao's numbers hardly reached 25 thousand in all. Bajirao repeatedly sent messages to Dabhade to solve the dispute amicably in the presence of Chatrapati Shahu. But Dabhade was stiff and stubborn, disagreeing with Bajirao's proposition, therefore on 1 April 1731, Bajirao struck at the allied forces of Dabhade, Gaekwad and Kadam Bande.

The Dabhade was seated on an elephant and Baji Rao was on horseback. But during the battle, a bullet pierced Trimbakrao's head and he died on the spot. Later it was discovered that the shot that killed Dabhade was fired by Dabhade's maternal uncle Bhau Singh Thoke. Baji Rao resolved the dispute with Sambhaji II on 13 April by signing the Treaty of Warna, which demarcated the territories of Shahu and Sambhaji II. The Nizam met Baji Rao at Rohe-Rameshwar on 27 December 1732, and promised not to interfere with Maratha expeditions.

Shahu and Baji Rao avoided a rivalry with the powerful Dabhade clan after subduing Trimbak Rao; Trimbak's son, Yashwant Rao, was appointed as Shahu's Senapati. The Dabhade clan was allowed to continue collecting Chauth from Gujarat if they deposited half the revenue in Shahu's treasury.

After the death of Trimbak Rao, Bangash's alliance against the Marathas fell apart. The Mughal emperor recalled him from Malwa and re-appointed Jai Singh II as governor of Malwa. However, the Maratha chief Holkar defeated Jai Singh in the 1733 Battle of Mandsaur. After two more battles, the Mughals decided to offer the Marathas the right to collect the equivalent of ?22 lakh in cChauthfrom Malwa. On 4 March 1736, Baji Rao and Jai Singh reached an agreement at Kishangad. Jai Singh convinced the emperor to agree to the plan, and Baji Rao was appointed deputy governor of the region.

The Peshwa began to march on the Mughal capital, Delhi, from Pune on 12 November 1736 with a force of 50,000 cavalry troops. Learning of the advancing Maratha army, the Mughal emperor asked Saadat Ali Khan I to march from Agra and check the advance. The Maratha chiefs Malhar Rao Holkar, Vithoji Bule and Pilaji Jadhav crossed the Yamuna and conquered the Mughal territories in the Doab. Saadat Khan led a force of 150,000, defeated them, and retired to Mathura. Malhar Rao Holkar rejoined Baji Rao's army near Gwalior. Samsam-ud-Daulah, Mir Bakshi and Muhammad Khan Bangash invited Saadat Ali Khan to a banquet in Samsam-ud-Daulah's tent in Mathura, thinking that the Marathas had retreated to the Deccan. During the feast, they learned that Baji Rao had slipped along the Jat and Mewati hill route (avoiding the direct Agra-Delhi route) and was at Delhi.

The Mughal commanders left the feast and began a hasty return to the capital. The Mughal emperor dispatched a force, led by Mir Hasan Khan Koka, to check Baji Rao's advance. The Marathas defeated his force in the 28 March 1737 Battle of Delhi. Baji Rao then retreated from the capital, concerned about the approach of a larger Mughal force from Mathura. Baji Rao's dash on Delhi was executed with such daring and audacity that neither the Mughal generals nor the Mughal intelligence could comprehend or predict his moves. Bajirao died of severe fever on 28 April 1740, at Raverkhedi on Narmada bank.

XII

Samudragupta

"A coward is incapable of exhibiting love; it is the prerogative of the brave." – Mahatma Gandhi

Samudragupta was a son of the Gupta emperor Chandragupta I and Queen Kumaradevi, who came from the Licchavi clan. His fragmentary Eran stone inscription states that his father selected him as the successor because of his "devotion, righteous conduct, and valour". His Allahabad Pillar inscription similarly describes how Chandragupta I called him a noble person in front of the courtiers and appointed him to "protect the earth". These descriptions suggest that Chandragupta I renounced the throne in his old age, and appointed his son as the next emperor.

The coins of a Gupta ruler named Kacha, whose identity is debated by modern scholars, describe him as "the exterminator of all kings". These coins closely resemble the coins issued by Samudragupta. According to one theory, Kacha was an earlier name of Samudragupta and the emperor later adopted the regnal name Samudra ("Ocean"), after extending his empire's dominion as far as the ocean. An alternative theory is that Kacha was a distinct king (possibly a rival claimant to the throne) who flourished before or after Samudragupta.

The Gupta inscriptions suggest that Samudragupta had a remarkable military career. The Eran stone inscription of Samudragupta states that he had brought "the whole tribe of kings" under his suzerainty and that his enemies were terrified when they thought of him in their dreams. The inscription does not name any of the defeated kings, but it suggests that Samudragupta had subdued several kings by this time. The later Allahabad Pillar inscription, a panegyric written by Samudragupta's minister and military officer Harishena, credits him with extensive conquests. It gives the most detailed account of Samudragupta's military conquests. It states that Samudragupta fought a hundred battles, acquired a hundred wounds that looked like marks of glory, and earned the title Prakrama (valourous). The Mathura stone inscription of Chandragupta II describes Samudragupta as an "exterminator of all kings", as someone who had no equally powerful enemy, and as a person whose "fame was tasted by the waters of the four oceans".

Modern scholars offer various opinions regarding Samudragupta's possible motivations behind his extensive military campaigns. The Allahabad Pillar inscription suggests that Samudragupta's aim was the unification of the earth (dharani-bandha), which suggests that he may have aspired to become a Chakravarti (a universal ruler). The Ashvamedha performances by the Nagas, whom he defeated, may have influenced him as well. His southern expedition may have been motivated by economic considerations of controlling the trade between India and South-East Asia.

The early portion of the Allahabad Pillar inscription mentions that Samudragupta "uprooted" Achyuta, Nagasena, and a ruler whose name is lost in the damaged portion of the inscription. The third name ends in "-ga", and is generally restored as Ganapati-naga, because Achyuta-nandin (presumably the same as Achyuta), Nagasena, and Ganapati-naga are once again mentioned in the later part of the inscription, among the kings of Aryavarta (northern India) defeated by Samudragupta. These kings are identified as the rulers of present-day western Uttar Pradesh. According to the inscription, Samudragupta reinstated these rulers after they sought his forgiveness.

It is not clear why the names of these three kings are repeated later in the inscription. According to one theory, these three kings were vassal rulers who rebelled against Samudragupta after the death of his father. Samudragupta crushed the rebellion, and reinstated them after they sought his forgiveness. Later, these rulers rebelled once more, and Samudragupta defeated them again. Another possibility is that the author of the inscription thought it necessary to repeat these names while describing Samudragupta's later conquests in Aryavarta, simply because these kings belonged to that region.

Samudragupta dispatched an army to capture the scion of the Kota family, whose identity is uncertain. The Kotas may have been the rulers of present-day Punjab, where coins bearing the legend "Kota", and featuring a symbol of Shiva and his bull, have been discovered.

The inscription states that the Gupta army captured the Kota ruler, while Samudragupta himself "played" (or pleased himself) in a city called Pushpa (the name Pushpa-pura referred to Pataliputra at Samudragupta's time, although it came to be used for Kanyakubja in the later period). Modern scholars have interpreted the word "played" in various ways: According to one theory, this portion describes Samudragupta's achievements as a prince. An alternative interpretation is that Samudragupta dispatched his army on these campaigns, while he himself stayed at the capital. It is also possible that the poet intended to convey that these campaigns were minor affairs that did not require the king's direct involvement at the battlefront.

Samudragupta's empire included a core territory, located in northern India, which was directly controlled by the emperor. Besides, it comprised a number of monarchical and tribal tributary states. Historian R. C. Majumdar theorizes that Samudragupta directly controlled an area extending from the Ravi River (Punjab) in the west to the Brahmaputra River (Bengal and Assam) in the east, and from the Himalayan foothills in the north to the Vindhya hills in the south. The south-western boundary of his territory roughly followed an imaginary line drawn from present-day Karnal to Bhilsa.

In the south, Samudragupta's empire definitely included Eran in present-day Madhya Pradesh, where his inscription has been found. The Allahabad Pillar inscription suggests that he advanced up to Kanchipuram in the south. However, the southern kings were not under his direct suzerainty: they only paid him tribute.

According to historian Kunal Chakrabarti, Samudragupta's military campaigns weakened the tribal republics of present-day Punjab and Rajasthan, but even these kingdoms were not under his direct suzerainty: they only paid him tribute. Samudragupta's claim of control over other kings is questionable. Historian Ashvini Agrawal notes that a gold coin of the Gadahara tribe bears the legend Samudra, which suggests that Samudragupta's control extended up to the Chenab river in the Punjab region.

The coinage of the Gupta Empire was initially derived from the coinage of the Kushan Empire, adopting its weight standard, techniques and designs, following the conquests of Samudragupta in the northwest of the subcontinent. The Guptas even adopted from the Kushans the name of Dinara for their coinage, which ultimately came from the Roman name Denarius aureus. The standard coin type of Samudragupta is highly similar to the coinage of the later Kushan rulers, including the sacrificial scene over an altar, and the depiction of a halo, while differences include the headdress of the ruler (a close-fitting cap instead of the Kushan pointed hat), the Garuda standard instead of the trident, and Samudragupta's jewelry, which is Indian.

Samudragupta was succeeded by Chandragupta II, who was his son from Dattadevi. Based on a reconstruction of the partially-lost Sanskrit play Devichandraguptam, a section of modern historians believe that Samudragupta was initially succeeded by Ramagupta (presumably the eldest son), who was then dethroned by

Chandragupta II.

XIII

Mihira Bhoj

"“When you work, work as if everything depends on you. When you pray, pray as if everything depends on God.” – J.R.D. Tata"

Mihira Bhoja or Bhoja I was a king belonging to the Gurjara-Pratihara Dynasty. He succeeded his father Ramabhadra. Bhoja was a devotee of Vishnu and adopted the title of Ādivarāha which is inscribed on some of his coins. One of the outstanding political figures of India in the ninth century, he ranks with Dhruva Dharavarsha and Dharmapala as a great general and empire builder.

At its height, Bhoja's empire extended to Narmada River in the South, Sutlej River in the northwest, and up to Bengal in the east. It extended over a large area from the foot of the Himalayas up to the river Narmada and included the present district of Etawah in Uttar Pradesh.

Mihira Bhoja first consolidated his territories by crushing the rebellious feudatories in Rajasthan, before turning his attention against the old enemies the Palas and Rastrakutas. The Palas of Bengal, ruled by King Devapala (c. 810–850), were reputed to have:

> *"Eradicated the race of the Utkalas, humbled the pride of the Hunas and scattered the conceit of the Dravidas and Pratiharas."-Badal Inscription."*

When Mihira Bhoja started his career reverses and defeats suffered by his father Ramabhadra had considerably lowered the prestige of the Royal family. He invaded the Pala Empire of Bengal but was defeated by Devapala

He then launched a campaign to conquer the territories to the south of his empire and was successful, Malwa, Deccan, and Gujarat were conquered. In Gujarat he Stepped into a war of succession for the throne of Gujarat between Dhruva II of the Gujarat Rashtrakuta dynasty and his younger brother, Bhoja led a cavalry raid into Gujarat against the Dhruva while supporting his Dhruva's younger brother. Although the raid was repulsed by Dhruva II. Bhoja was able to retain dominion over parts of Gujarat and Malwa.

The Pratiharas were defeated in a large battle in Ujjain by Rastrakutas of Gujarat however, retribution followed on the part of the Pratiharas, and by the end of his reign, Bhoja had successfully destroyed the Gujarat Rashtrakuta dynasty.

Bhoja's feudatory, the Guhilas chief named Harsha of Chatsu, is described as :

> *""Defeating the northern rulers with the help of the mighty elephant force", and "loyally presenting to Bhoja the special 'Shrivamsha' breed of horses, which could easily cross seas of sand." He gradually rebuilt the empire by conquest of territories in Rajputana, Gujarat , and Madhya Pradesh"*

The Kingdoms which were conquered and acknowledged his suzerainty includes Travani, Valla, Mada, Arya, Gujarat, Lata Parvarta, and Chandelas of Bundelkhand. Bhoja's Daulatpura-Dausa Inscription(AD 843), confirms his rule in the Dausa region. Another inscription states that "Bhoja's territories extended to the east of the Sutlej river."

Kalhana's Rajatarangini states that the territories of Bhoja extended to Kashmir in the north, and bhoja had conquered Punjab by defeating the ruling 'Thakkiyaka' dynasty. After Devapala's death, Bhoja defeated the Pala King Narayanapala and expanded his boundaries eastward into Pala-held territories near Gorakhpur.

Hudud-ul-Alam a tenth-century Persian geographic text states that most of the kings of India acknowledged the supremacy of the powerful 'Rai of Qinnauj', (kannauj was the capital of Imperial Pratiharas) whose mighty army had 150,000 strong cavalry and 800 war elephants. His son Mahenderpal I (890–910), expanded further eastwards in Magadha, Bengal, and Assam.

XIV
Hemchandra

"Depth of friendship does not depend on the length of acquaintance." – Rabindranath Tagore

Details of Hemu's early career are vague and involve much speculation. After Sher Shah Suri's death in 1545, his son Islam Shah became the ruler of the Sur Empire and during his rule, Hemu rose to become the superintendent of the market in Delhi with some soldierly experience under his belt. Hemu is subsequently said to have been appointed the Chief of Intelligence and Superintendent of Posts. Other sources also place him as a surveyor of the imperial kitchens.

Islam Shah, who liked to place Hindus in command alongside Afghan officers so that they could spy on each other, recognized Hemu's soldierly qualities and assigned him responsibilities equivalent to those of a high-ranking officer. Hemu was then dispatched to monitor the movements of Humayun's half-brother, Kamran Mirza, in the neighborhood of Mankot.

Islam Shah died on 30 October 1553 and was succeeded by his 12-year-old son, Firoz Khan, who was killed within three days of his accession by his uncle, Adil Shah Suri. The new ruler was however more interested in the pursuit of pleasure than affairs of the state.

But Hemu threw in his lot with Adil Shah and his military successes led him to be elevated to the position of Chief Minister and the general supervisor of the state. According to Abu'l-Fazl, Hemu "undertook all appointments and dismissals, and the distribution of justice" in the Shah's court.

Hemu, besides being a highly capable civil administrator, was also the finest military mind on the Afghan side after the demise of Sher Shah Suri. He is reputed to have waged and won as many as 22 battles against the opponents of Adil Shah. Many of these battles were against Afghans who had rebelled against Adil Shah. One of these was Taj Khan Karrani, a member of Islam Shah's court who, rather than serving Adil Shah, decided to flee with his followers from Gwalior towards the east. He was overtaken by Hemu at Chibramau and defeated, but somehow managed to escape and plundered and robbed his way to Chunar. Hemu gave chase again and fought Karrani at Chunar and was victorious once more. However, just as at Chibramau, Karrani gave him the slip again. Hemu asked Adil Shah—who had accompanied him—to remain at Chunar and proceeded to chase Karrani all the way to Bengal.

After the victory of Humayun over Adil Shah's brother-in-law, Sikandar Shah Suri, on 23 July 1555, the Mughals finally recovered Delhi and Agra. Hemu was in Bengal when Humayun died on 26 January 1556. His death gave Hemu an ideal opportunity to defeat the Mughals. He started a rapid march from Bengal and drove the Mughals out of Bayana, Etawah, Sambhal, Kalpi, and Narnaul. In Agra, the governor evacuated the city and fled without a fight upon hearing of Hemu's invasion.

Tardi Beg Khan, who was Akbar's governor in Delhi, wrote to his masters who were camped at Jalandhar, that Hemu had captured Agra and intended to attack the capital Delhi which could not be defended without reinforcements. While the main army could not be spared due to the belligerent presence of Sikandar Shah Suri, Akbar's regent, Bairam Khan, realizing the gravity of the situation, sent his most capable lieutenant, Pir Muhammad Sharwani, to Delhi. Meanwhile, Tardi Beg Khan had also ordered all the Mughal nobles in the vicinity to muster their forces at Delhi. A council of war was convened where it was decided that the Mughals would stand and fight Hemu, and plans were made accordingly.

After winning Agra, Hemu, who had set off in pursuit of the city's governor, reached Tughlaqabad, a village just outside Delhi where he ran into Tardi Beg Khan's forces. The Mughals while outnumbered, put up a gallant fight against Hemu's forces which, according to Bada'uni, included 1000 elephants, 50,000 horses, 51 cannon and 500 falconets. Jadunath Sarkar describes the battle thus:

The Mughal army was thus drawn up: Abdullah Uzbeg commanded the Van, Haidar Muhammad on the right wing, Iskandar Beg on the left, and Tardi Beg himself on the center The choice Turki cavalry in the van and left-wing attacked and drove back the enemy forces before them, and followed far in pursuit. In this assault the victors captured 400 elephants and slew 3,000 men of the Afghan army. Imagining victory already gained, many of Tardi Beg's followers dispersed to plunder the enemy camp, and he was left in the field very thinly guarded. All this time Hemu had been holding 300 choice elephants and a force of select horsemen as a reserve in the center. He promptly seized the opportunity and made a sudden charge upon Tardi Beg with this reserve. At the impetuous advance of the huge beasts and the dense cavalry behind them, many of the Mughal officers fled away in terror without waiting to offer a defense. At last Tardi Beg himself took the same course.

Hemu's push was also bolstered by the timely arrival of fresh reinforcements from Alwar under the command of Haji Khan. When the previously victorious Mughal vanguard and left wing returned from their pursuit, they realised that the day was lost and dispersed without offering a fight. Hemu took possession of Delhi after a day's battle on 7 October 1556.

After taking control of Delhi, Hemu claimed royal status and assumed the title of Vikramaditya (or Bikramjit), an appellation used by a number of Hindu kings in India's ancient past. What this signifies is, however, a subject of speculation among historians.

Historians such as Satish Chandra do not believe that this implies that Hemu had declared himself to be an independent king. He reasons that, for one, none of the Mughal authors of the time explicitly say so in their histories. In the Akbarnama, Abu'l-Fazl writes that after Hemu's victory at Tughlaqabad, "the ambition of sovereignty" was stirring within him. According to Bada'uni, Hemu took on the title of Bikramjit like a great Raja of Hindustan. Another contemporary historian named Nizamuddin Ahmad merely states that Hemu took on the said title, but refrains from saying anything more. Secondly, it would have been an ill-advised move as Hemu's military force was composed almost entirely of Afghans. According to Bada'uni, there were also some murmurings against Hemu amongst the Afghans who were "sick of his usurpation ... prayed for his downfall".

Other historians describe Hemu's claim to be an attempt to set himself up as an independent ruler, throwing off the yoke of Adil Shah's authority. Abraham Eraly quotes Ahmad Yadgar[19] who states in his history of the Afghans that Hemu "raised the imperial canopy over him, and ordered coin to be struck in his name". This was done in connivance with the Afghans to whom he had liberally distributed the spoils.

Whether he had set himself up as an independent king or not, Hemu Vikramaditya's reign was to be short-lived as he would again clash with the Mughals only a month later. This time the battlefield would be at Panipat, not far from the site where Akbar's grandfather, Babur, had been victorious against the Lodis 30 years earlier.

On hearing the disastrous news from Tughlaqabad, Akbar immediately set off for Delhi. Ali Quli Khan Shaibani who had been sent ahead with a 10,000-strong cavalry force chanced upon Hemu's artillery which was being transported under a weak guard. He was easily able to capture the entire train of artillery. This would prove to be a costly loss for Hemu.

On 5 November 1556, the Mughal army met Hemu's army at the historic battlefield of Panipat. Akbar and Bairam Khan stayed in the rear, eight miles from the battleground. The Mughal army was led by Ali Quli Khan Shaibani in the center with Sikandar Khan Uzbak on the right and Abdulla Khan Uzbak on the left and the vanguard led by Husain Quli Beg and Shah Quli Mahram. Hemu led his army himself into battle, atop an elephant named Hawai. His left was led by his sister's son, Ramya, and the right by Shadi Khan Kakkar. It was a desperately contested battle but the advantage tilted in favour of Hemu. Both the wings of the Mughal army had been driven back and Hemu moved his contingent of war elephants and cavalry forward to crush their centre. Hemu was on the cusp of victory when he was wounded in the eye by a Mughal arrow and collapsed unconscious. This triggered a panic in his army which broke formation and fled. The battle was lost; 5000 dead lay on the field of battle and many more were killed while fleeing.

The elephant carrying the wounded Hemu was captured and led to the Mughal camp. Bairam Khan asked the 13-year-old Akbar to behead Hemu. According to Akbar's later courtier Abu'l-Fazl ibn Mubarak, he refused to take the sword to a dead man. However, this is not attested by contemporary writer Muhammad Arif Qandhari (composed Tarikh e Akbari) who mentioned that Akbar followed Bairam Khan's advice and himself beheaded Hemu and took the title of Ghazi. The account of Akbar's refusal to behead Hemu is probably a later invention of his courtiers. Hemu's head was sent to Kabul while his body was gibbeted on a gate in Delhi. A minaret was subsequently constructed of the heads of the other dead.

XV

Guru Tegh Bahadur

"A mind all logic is like a knife all blade. It makes the hand bleed that uses it." – Rabindranath Tagore

Guru Tegh Bahadur was the ninth of ten Gurus who founded the Sikh religion and the leader of Sikhs from 1665 until his beheading in 1675. Guru Tegh Bahadur was the youngest son of Guru Hargobind, the sixth guru: Guru Hargobind had one daughter, Bibi Viro, and five sons: Baba Gurditta, Suraj Mal, Ani Rai, Atal Rai, and Tyaga Mal. Tyaga Mal was born in Amritsar in the early hours of 1 April 1621. He came to be known by the name Tegh Bahadur (Mighty of the Sword), given to him by Guru Hargobind after he had shown his valor in a battle against the Mughals.

Amritsar at that time was the center of the Sikh faith. As the seat of the Sikh Gurus, and with its connection to Sikhs in far-flung areas of the country through the chains of Masands or missionaries, it had developed the characteristics of a state capital. Guru Tegh Bahadur was brought up in the Sikh culture and trained in archery and horsemanship. He was also taught the old classics such as the Vedas, the Upanishads, and the Puranas. Tegh Bahadur was married on 3 February 1632 to Mata Gujri.

In March 1664, Guru Har Krishan contracted smallpox. When asked by his followers who would lead them after him, he replied Baba Bakala, meaning his successor was to be found in Bakala. Taking advantage of the ambiguity in the words of the dying Guru, many installed themselves in Bakala, claiming themselves as the new Guru. Sikhs were puzzled to see so many claimants.

Sikh tradition has a myth concerning the manner in which Tegh Bahadur was selected as the ninth guru. A wealthy trader, Baba Makhan Shah Labana, had once prayed for his life and had promised to gift 500 gold coins to the Sikh Guru if he survived. He arrived in search of the ninth Guru. He went from one claimant to the next making his obeisance and offering two gold coins to each Guru, believing that the right guru would know that his silent promise was to gift 500 coins for his safety. Every "guru" he met accepted the two gold coins and bid him farewell. Then he discovered that Tegh Bahadur also lived at Bakala. Labana gifted Tegh Bahadur the usual offering of two gold coins. Tegh Bahadur gave him his blessings and remarked that his offering was considerably short of the promised five hundred. Makhan Shah Labana forthwith made good the difference and ran upstairs. He began shouting from the rooftop, "Guru ladho re, Guru ladho re" meaning "I have found the Guru, I have found the Guru".

In August 1664, a Sikh Sangat arrived in Bakala and appointed Tegh Bahadur as the ninth guru of Sikhs. The Sangat was led by Diwan Durga Mal, elder brother of Guru Tegh Bahadur, conferring Guruship on Him. As had been the custom among Sikhs after the execution of Guru Arjan by Mughal Emperor Jahangir, Guru Tegh Bahadur was surrounded by armed bodyguards.

Guru Tegh Bahadur traveled extensively in different parts of the country, including Dhaka and Assam, to preach the teachings of Nanak, the first Sikh guru. The places he visited and stayed in became sites of Sikh temples. During his travels, Guru Tegh Bahadur spread the Sikh ideas and message, as well as started community water wells and langars (community kitchen charity for the poor).

The Guru made three successive visits to Kiratpur. On 21 August 1664, Guru Tegh Bahadur went there to console Bibi Roop upon the death of her father, Guru Har Rai, the seventh Sikh guru, and of his brother, Guru Har Krishan. The second visit was on 15 October 1664, at the death on 29 September 1664, of Bassi, the mother of Guru Har Rai. A third visit concluded a fairly extensive journey through the northwest Indian subcontinent. His son Guru Gobind Singh, who would be the tenth Sikh Guru, was born in Patna, while he was away in Dhubri, Assam in 1666, where stands the Gurdwara Sri Guru Tegh Bahadur Sahib. There he helped end the war between Raja Ram Singh of Bengal and Raja Chakardwaj of Ahom state (later Assam). He visited the towns of Mathura, Agra, Allahabad and Varanasi.

After his visit to Assam, Bengal and Bihar, the Guru visited Rani Champa of Bilaspur who offered to give the Guru a piece of land in her state. The Guru bought the site for 500 rupees. There, Guru Tegh Bahadur founded the city of Anandpur Sahib in the foothills of Himalayas. In 1672, Tegh Bahadur traveled through Kashmir and the North-West Frontier, to meet the masses, as the persecution of non-Muslims reached new heights.

Guru Tegh Bahadur's son and successor recalled Guru's execution:

> "*In this dark age, Tegh Bahadur performed a great act of chivalry (saka) for the sake of the frontal mark and sacred thread. He offered all he had for the holy. He gave up his head, but did not utter a sigh. He suffered martyrdom for the sake of religion. He laid down his head, but not his honor. Real men of god do not perform tricks like showmen. Having broken the pitcher on the head of the king of Delhi, he departed to the world of god. No one has ever performed a deed like him. At his departure, the whole world mourned, while the heavens hailed it as victory.*
>
> *— Guru Gobind Singh*"

More Sikh accounts of Tegh Bahadur's execution, all claiming to be sourced from the "testimony of trustworthy Sikhs", only started emerging in around the late eighteenth century, and are thus, often conflicting. Chronicler Sohan Lal Suri states that the Guru gained thousands of followers of soldiers and horsemen during his travels between 1672 and 1673 in southern Punjab and provided shelter to those who were resistant to Mughal representatives. Aurangzeb was warned about such activity, as a cause of concern that could possibly lead to rebellion.

Persian sources maintain that the Guru was a bandit whose plunder and rapine of Punjab along with his rebellious activities precipitated his execution. The earliest Persian source to chronicle his execution is Siyar-ul-Mutakhkherin by Ghulam Hussain Khan c. 1782, where Tegh Bahadur's (alleged) oppression of subjects is held to have incurred Aurangzeb's wrath:

> "*Tegh Bahadur, the Ninth successor of (Guru) Nanak became a man of authority with a large number of followers. (In fact) Several thousand persons used to accompany him as he moved from place to place. His contemporary Hafiz Adam, a faqir belonging to the group of Shaikh Ahmad Sirhindi's followers, had also come to have a large number of murids and followers. Both these men (Guru Tegh Bahadur and Hafiz Adam) used to move about in Punjab, adopting a habit of coercion and extortion. Tegh Bahadur used to collect money from Hindus and Hafiz Adam from Muslims. The royal waqia navis (news reporter and intelligence agent) wrote to Emperor Alamgir Aurangzeb about their manner of activity and added that if their authority increased they could become even refractory.*
>
> *— Ghulam Husain, Siyar-ul-Mutakhkherin*"

Satish Chandra however cautions against taking Hussain Khan's argument at face value. He was a relative of Alivardi Khan — one of the closest confidantes of Aurangzeb — and might have been providing an "official justification". There are other challenges to the above narrative. Ghulam Husain lived far away from Punjab. Also, the Guru's association with Hafiz Adam is anachronistic. Hafiz Adam died in Medina in A.D. 1643, 21 years before Tegh Bahadur attained the status of Guru. Further, it should be pointed out that according to Ghulam Husain, Tegh Bahadur was confined in Gwalior, where, under imperial orders, his body was "cut into four quarters" and hung at the four gates of the fortress while it is well known that Tegh Bahadur was executed in Delhi where the Sisganj Gurudwara is situated at present.

The Sikh Sakhis written during the eighteenth century indirectly support the narrative in the Persian sources; nothing that the Guru was in "violent opposition to the Muslim rulers of the country" in response to the dogmatic policies implemented by Aurangzeb. Both Persian and Sikh sources agree that Tegh Bahadur militarily opposed the Mughal state and was therefore targeted for execution in accordance with Aurangzeb's zeal for punishing enemies of the state.

Many scholars identify the narrative as follows: A congregation of Hindu Pandits from Kashmir requested help against Aurangzeb's oppressive policies, to which Guru Tegh Bahadur decided to protect their rights. Tegh Bahadur left from his base at Makhowal to confront the persecution of Kashmiri Brahmins by Mughal officials but was arrested at Ropar and put in jail in Sirhind. Four months later, in November 1675, he was transferred to Delhi and asked to perform a miracle to prove his nearness to God or convert to Islam.[39] The Guru declined and three of his colleagues, who had been arrested with him, were tortured to death in front of him: Bhai Mati Das was sawn into pieces, Bhai Dayal Das was thrown into a cauldron of boiling water, and Bhai Sati Das was burned alive. Thereafter, Tegh Bahadur was publicly beheaded in Chandni Chowk, a market square close to the Red Fort.

Satish Chandra expresses doubt about the authenticity of these meta-narratives, centered on miracles — Aurangzeb was not a believer in them. He further expresses doubt pertaining to the narrative of the persecution of Hindus in Kashmir within Sikh accounts, remarking that no contemporary sources mentioned the persecution of Hindus there. Louis Fenech refuses to pass any judgment, in light of the paucity of primary sources; however, he notes that these Sikh accounts had coded martyrdom into the events, with an aim to elicit pride than trauma in readers. He further argues that Tegh Bahadur had sacrificed himself for the sake of his own faith; the janju and tilak in the passage in the Bachittar Natak refer to his own.

Remarkably, in contrast to this dominating theme in Sikh literature, some pre-modern Sikh accounts had laid the blame on an acrimonious succession dispute: Ram Rai, elder brother of Guru Har Krishan, was held to have instigated Aurangzeb against Tegh Bahadur by suggesting that he prove his spiritual greatness by performing miracles at the Court. Sohan Lal Suri, the court historian of Ranjit Singh, in his magisterial Umdat ut Tawarikh (c. 1805) chose to reiterate Hussain Khan's argument at large: Tegh Bahadur had provided refuge to all classes of rebels and commanded a huge nomadic army across Punjab; so he was put down at the earliest, lest he declares an insurrection in near future.

Chandragupta Maurya stamp issued by the Government of India.

King Porus (on elephant) fighting Alexander the Great, on a "victory coin" of Alexander (minted c. 324–322 BC)

1st century BCE/CE relief from Sanchi, showing Ashoka on his chariot, visiting the Nagas at Ramagrama.

Coin of Harshavardhana, circa 606–647 CE

The Kanishka statue in the Mathura Museum.

A Mural of Rajaraja I with his guru Karuvurar at Brihadisvara Temple.

A portrait of Krishnadevaraya by Portuguese traveler Domingo Paes c. 16th century

Statue of Prithviraj Chauhan at Ajmer

Court of Pulakeshin II

Portrait of Pratap by Raja Ravi Varma

Shivaji's portrait (1680s) from the collection of the British Museum

Portrait of Baji Rao I c.18th century

Coin of Samudragupta, with Garuda pillar, emblem of Gupta Empire.

Pushyamitra Shunga

Raja Dahir Sen of Sindh

Restored impression of Martand Surya Mandir built by Lalitaditya Muktapida

Gold coin of Skandagupta, depicting himself on the obverse, Lakshmi on the reverse.

Telika Mandir built by Mihira Bhoj

Portrayal of Hemu Vikramaditya

A mid-17th century portrait of Guru Tegh Bahadur painted by Ahsan

Rani Chenamma

Bibliography

Chapter 1: Chandragupta Maurya

- Britannica, The Editors of Encyclopaedia. "Chandragupta". Encyclopedia Britannica, 23 Jan. 2020, https://www.britannica.com/biography/Chandragupta. Accessed 12 June 2022.
- Lal, Dr. Avantika. "Chandragupta Maurya." World History Encyclopedia. World History Encyclopedia, 04 Feb 2019. Web. 12 Jun 2022.
- Lal, D. K. (2018). Brihat Bharat Ka Nirmata Chandragupta Maurya. Prabhat Prakashan.

Chapter 2: Porus

- Khan, S. (n.d.). Mighty Porus and Alexander The Great: The Clash of Two Giants.
- Trivedi, B. (2020). Mighty Porus and Alexander The Great: The Clash of Two Giants. Samvedna Shiksha.
- Britannica, T. Editors of Encyclopaedia (2020, April 3). Porus. Encyclopedia Britannica. https://www.britannica.com/biography/Porus
- Livius Org. (2002). Porus. Livius. Retrieved June 18, 2022, from https://www.livius.org/articles/person/porus/
- Wasson, D. L. (2014, February 26). Battle of Hydaspes. World History Encyclopedia. Retrieved from https://www.worldhistory.org/article/660/battle-of-hydaspes/
- Gill, N. S. (2020, January 28). Alexander the Great fought this king of India. ThoughtCo. Retrieved June 18, 2022, from

https://www.thoughtco.com/king-porus-of-paurava-116851

- Plutarch. "Plutarch, Alexander,Chapter 60." Plutarch, Alexander,Chapter 60, www.perseus.tufts.edu, http://www.perseus.tufts.edu/hopper/text?doc=Perseus:abo:tlg,0007,047:60. Accessed 25 June 2022.

Chapter 3: Harshavardhana

- Sharma, Yagya. Harsha: The Gallant King of Kanauj. Amar Chitra Katha Pvt. Ltd., 1972.
- Mookerji, Radha Kumud. Harsha. Motilal Banarasidass, 2006.
- Britannica, The Editors of Encyclopaedia. "Harsha". Encyclopedia Britannica, 27 Apr. 2021, https://www.britannica.com/biography/Harsha. Accessed 26 June 2022.
- Chugani, Gaurav. "Harsha." World History Encyclopedia. World History Encyclopedia, 14 Mar 2016. Web. 26 Jun 2022.
- Banabhatta, et al. The Harshacharita. Global Vision Publishing House, 2017.

Chapter 4: Kanishka

- Singh, Bittu K. Kanishka: A Great Commander. Bhairavi Publisher, 2018.
- Britannica, The Editors of Encyclopaedia. "Kaniska". Encyclopedia Britannica, 4 Apr. 2019, https://www.britannica.com/biography/Kaniska. Accessed 1 July 2022.
- "Kanishka." Columbia University, http://www.columbia.edu/itc/mealac/pritchett/00routesdata/0100_0199/kanishka/kanishka.html. Accessed 1 July 2022.

- "Kanishka ." Encyclopedia of World Biography. . Encyclopedia.com. 21 Jun. 2022 <https://www.encyclopedia.com>.
- “Kanishka.” Nichiren Buddhism Library, www.nichirenlibrary.org/en/dic/Content/K/26. Accessed 1 July 2022.
- Basham, Arthur L., Papers on the Date of Kanishka, E. J. Brill (Leiden, Netherlands), 1968.

Chapter 5: Prithviraj Chauhan

- “Prithviraja III | Rajput Chauhan King.” Encyclopedia Britannica, www.britannica.com, https://www.britannica.com/biography/Prithviraja-III. Accessed 27 July 2022.
- “Prithviraj Chauhan: सम्राट पृथ्वीराज चौहान की कहानी: कल्पना कितनी, हक़ीक़त कितनी? (BBC Hindi).” YouTube, www.youtube.com, 5 June 2022, https://www.youtube.com/watch?v=JOIwe5Lt2tE.
- Sharma, Yagya. Prithviraj Chauhan. Amar Chitra Katha Private Limited, 1972.
- Rathore, Virendra Singh. Prithviraj Chauhan – A Light on the Mist in History. White Falcon Publishing, 2020.

Chapter 6: Raja Dahir

- Arya, D. R. K. (2021). Rashtranayak Raja Dahir Sen. Diamond Books.
- Khushalani, G. (2006). Chachnamah Retold: An Account of the Arab Conquest of Sindh. Bibliophile South Asia.
- Murthy, P. A. V. N. (2020, February 23). King Raja Dahir: Forgotten Hero. Star of Mysore. Retrieved June 16, 2022, from https://starofmysore.com/king-raja-dahir-forgotten-hero/

Chapter 7: Lalitaditya Muktapida

- Sonawani, S. (2019). Emperor of Kashmir: Lalitaditya the great. Chinar Publishers.
- Stein, M. A. (2019). Kalhana's Rajatarangini: A Chronicle of the Kings of Kashmir. New Bharatiya Book Corporation.
- Sharma, Y., Waeerkar, R., & Pai, A. (2011). The legend of lalitaditya: The warrior-poet of Kashmir. Amar Chitra Katha, ACK Media.
- Raina, G. L. (2021, July 28). Remembering Lalitaditya: The great emperor from Kashmir. Rising Kashmir. Retrieved June 17, 2022, from https://www.risingkashmir.com/Remembering-Lalitaditya--The-Great-Emperor-from-Kashmir-77435

Chapter 8: Maharana Pratap

- Britannica, The Editors of Encyclopaedia. "Rana Pratap Singh". Encyclopedia Britannica, 15 Jan. 2022, https://www.britannica.com/biography/Rana-Pratap-Singh. Accessed 24 July 2022.
- Hooja, Rima. Maharana Pratap: The Invincible Warrior. Juggernaut, 2019.
- Bandyopadhyay, Brishti. Maharana Pratap: Mewar's Rebel King. Rupa Publications India, 2007.
- Satish Chandra (2007). History of Medieval India:800-1700. Orient Longman. p. 231. ISBN 978-81-250-3226-7. When the Mughals stormed the fort, these peasants and many of the Rajput warriors amounting to 30,000 were massacred the first time Akbar indulged in such carnage. The Rajput warriors died after extracting as much vengeance as possible."

Chapter 9: Raja Raja Chola

- "Raja Raja Chola I - New World Encyclopedia." Raja Raja Chola I - New World Encyclopedia, www.newworldencyclopedia.org, https://www.newworldencyclopedia.org/entry/Raja_Raja_Chola_I.
- Anantharaman, Sita. Raja Raja Chola. Amar Chitra Katha Private Limited.
- Srinivasan, Raghavan. Rajaraja Chola: Interplay Between an Imperial Regime and Productive Forces of Society. One Point Six Technologies Pvt Ltd.

Chapter 10: Krishnadevaraya

- Reddy, Srinivas. "RAYA: Krishnadevaraya of Vijayanagara." Juggernaut.
- Chandrakant, Kamala. Krishnadeva Raya. Amar Chitra Katha.

Chapter 11: Peshwa Bajirao

- Joglekar, Anagdha. Bajirao Ballal: Ek Advitiya Yoddha. Notion Press.

Chapter 12: Samudragupta

- Sengupta, Nandini. The Ocean's Own. HarperCollins India, 2021.

Chapter 13: Mihira Bhoj

- "Mihira Bhoja | King of Pratihāra." Encyclopedia Britannica, www.britannica.com, https://www.britannica.com/biography/Mihira-Bhoja. Accessed 11 Aug. 2022.

Chapter 14: Hemchandra

- "Hemu: A National Freedom Fighter & the Hero of 2nd Battle of Panipat | Panipat, Haryana | India." Hemu: A National Freedom Fighter & the Hero of 2nd Battle of Panipat | Panipat, Haryana | India, panipat.gov.in, https://panipat.gov.in/hemu-a-national-freedom-fighter-the-hero-of-2nd-battle-of-panipat/. Accessed 11 Aug. 2022.

Chapter 15: Guru Tegh Bahadur

- Britannica, The Editors of Encyclopaedia. "Guru Tegh Bahādur". Encyclopedia Britannica, 7 Mar. 2022, https://www.britannica.com/biography/Guru-Tegh-Bahadur. Accessed 11 August 2022.

About The Author

Arin Kumar Shukla FRAS is an Indian author and columnist. He was born on the 25th of October, 2005. He writes on Indian history, politics, mythology, and global affairs. He is a vocal supporter of cultural rejuvenation in India. He is also an elected fellow of the Royal Asiatic Society of Great Britain and Ireland. In 2022, he was awarded IBR Award for his book "Greatest Stories of Indian Mythology". His works are applauded by many academicians and readers globally.

Printed by Libri Plureos GmbH in Hamburg,
Germany